Directing the Play

Tekena Gasper Mark

Rivers State University, Nigeria

Series in Performing Arts

VERNON PRESS

www.vernonpress.com

In the Americas:
Vernon Press
1000 N West Street, Suite 1200
Wilmington, Delaware, 19801
United States

In the rest of the world:
Vernon Press
C/Sancti Espiritu 17,
Malaga, 29006
Spain

Series in Performing Arts

Library of Congress Control Number: 2023936069

ISBN: 978-1-64889-909-6

Also available: 978-1-64889-672-9 [Hardback]; 978-1-64889-759-7 [PDF, E-Book]

Cover design by Vernon Press. Cover image: *The Struggle,* Port Harcourt, 2022 (ig@ambassadors_shot).

Dedication

This book is dedicated to the God almighty who gave me the insight, grace, and patience to realize this vision.

Acknowledgements

My academic grandfather and boss, the late Professor Samuel Ukala, did an incredible amount of work for me, and I will always be grateful to him for that. Sir, your suggestions and editing significantly raised the calibre of this work. Continue to rest in the bosom of the Lord.

To Professors Emmanuel Calvin Emasealu, Henry Leopold Bell-Gam, Clive Krama, Innocent Ohiri, Friday Nwafor, Innocent Uwah, Alex Asigbo, Femi Shaka, Julie Umukoro, Julie Okoh, Faith Ibarakumo Ken-Aminikpo, and Benjamin Ejiofor, God bless you for letting me drink from your well of academic knowledge and experience. My gratitude goes to Dr. Anyanwu, Remigius Anayochi, Dr. Imo Edward, Dr. Edum Sunday, Dr. Richard Iloma, Mr. Daniel Kpodoh, Mr. Patrick Bira and other members of staff of the Department of Theatre and Film Studies, University of Port Harcourt.

I want to thank my mother, Mrs. Boma Mark, my sisters, Hilda and Esther, and my brothers, Daniel and Victor, for supporting me and being my backbone. I sincerely appreciate your prayers, words of encouragement, and support. To my friends, Dr. Mrs. Pamela Chima, Dr. Mrs. Chidinma Lilian Agogbuo, Lekia Osaro, Gloria Umorem, Eke Princewill Ogbobuike, Divine Kara, Cyril Bieh, and Barthram Kenneth, God bless you all.

Table of Contents

Dedication   **iii**

Acknowledgements   **v**

List of Figures   **xi**

Foreword   **xiii**

Chapter 1   **Introduction**   1
            Background to the Study
            Aim and Objectives of the Study
            Rationale for the Study
            Significance of the Study
            Research Method
            Definition of Operational Terms

Chapter 2   **History, Qualities, Tools, Types and
            Functions of the Director**   7
            Development of Directing
            Qualities of the Director
            The Director's Tools
            Types of Directors
            Functions of the Director

Chapter 3   **Principles of Directing**   19
            Composition
            Picturization
            Movement
            Rhythm
            Pantomimic Dramatization

Chapter 4   **Western Theories of Directing**   31

George II, Duke of Saxe-Meiningen, and
His "Pictorial Motion and Ensemble Playing"
Technique

Constantin Stanislavski and His "The System"
Technique

Jerzy Grotowski and His "Poor Theatre"
Technique

Chapter 5   **West African Directors and their Techniques**   41

Ola Rotimi and His "Pressure Cooker, Festival
Theatre and Convoluting Concourse of Variegated
Happenings" Technique

Sam Ukala and His "Folkism" Technique

Dapo Adelugba and His "Dauduism or
Adelugbaresque" Technique

Henry Leopold Bell-Gam and His "Aquatic
Theatre" Technique

Effiong Johnson and His "Impact-Contact
Aesthetics" Technique

AbdulRasheed Abiodun Adeoye and His
"Neo-Alienation Aesthetics" Technique

Sunday Enessi Ododo and His *Facekuerade*
Theatre" Technique

Inih Akpan Ebong and His "Cosmo-Humo
Symbiosis" Technique

Efua Theodora Sutherland and Her "Anansegoro"
Technique

Chapter 6   **Directors from South Africa, North Africa,
East Africa, and their Techniques**   63

Bheki Mkhwane and His "Workshop and Physical
Theatre" Technique

Fadhel Jaibi and His "Poetics of Confrontation"
Technique

Joseph Murungu and His "Improvisational
Directing" Technique

Chapter 7   **The Development of the Theatre Stage**   73

Historical Development of the Theatre Stage

The Stage in Classical Greece (Fifth – Fourth
Century BC) and Roman Era (Fifth Century BC)

The Stage in the Middle Ages (Fifth – Fifteenth
Centuries)

The Stage in Renaissance England - The Apron
Stage (Late Fifteenth - Early Sixteenth Centuries)

The Stage in the Restoration Period -The Restoration
Stage (Seventeenth – Eighteenth Centuries)

The Stage in Modern Times -The Proscenium Stage
(Nineteenth – Twentieth Centuries)

The Development of the African/Nigerian Theatre
Stage

Chapter 8   **Directing on the Arena Stage**   81

Characteristics of the Arena Stage

Advantages of the Arena Stage

Disadvantages of the Arena Stage

Directorial Implications of the Arena Stage

Chapter 9   **Directing on the Proscenium Stage**   85

Characteristics of the Proscenium Stage

Advantages of the Proscenium Stage

Disadvantages of the Proscenium Stage

Directorial Implications of the Proscenium Stage

Chapter 10   **Directing on the Thrust Stage**   93

Characteristics of the Thrust Stage

Advantages of the Thrust Stage

Disadvantages of the Thrust Stage

Directorial Implications of the Thrust Stage

Chapter 11   **Directing on the Traverse Stage**   97

Characteristics of the Traverse Stage

Advantages of the Traverse Stage

Disadvantages of the Traverse Stage

Directorial Implications of the Traverse Stage

Chapter 12   **Directing on the African Traditional Theatre Stage**   101

Characteristics of the African Traditional Theatre Stage

Advantages of the African Traditional Theatre Stage

Disadvantages of the African Traditional Theatre Stage

Directorial Implications of the African Traditional Theatre Stage

Chapter 13   **Blocking and Movement**   111

Movement and Physical Behaviour of Characters

Stage Orientations and Emphasis

Body Positions

Blocking Positions

Acknowledgement and Support

Implementing Choices

Stage versus Screen Blocking

Chapter 14   **Directorial Concept and Directorial Approach**   123

Directorial Concept

Directional Approach

Conclusion   **127**

List of References   **129**

About the Author   **135**

Index   **137**

List of Figures

Figure 3.1:	Use of composition in the production of Ahmed Yerima's *Hard Ground*	20
Figure 3.2:	Use of composition in Scene Two	21
Figure 3.3:	Use of blocking in the production of Ahmed Yerima's *Hard Ground*	23
Figure 3.4:	Circular Formation	24
Figure 3.5:	Zig-Zag Formation	25
Figure 3.6:	Serpentine Formation	25
Figure 3.7:	The Straight line Formation	25
Figure 3.8:	Curve Formation	26
Figure 3.9:	Arc Formation	26
Figures 3.10 & 3.11: Angular Formations		26
Figures 3.12 & 3.13: Square Formation		27
Figure 3.14:	Diagonal Formation	27
Figure 3.15:	Levels of Movement	28
Figure 3.16:	Directions of Movement	28
Figure 7.1:	The Greek Theatre	74
Figure 7.2:	Roman Theatre	74
Figure 7.3:	The Medieval Stage	75
Figure 7.4:	The Elizabethan Theatre	76
Figure 7.5:	The Restoration Stage	77
Figure 7.6:	The Proscenium Theatre	78
Figure 8.1:	The Arena Stage	82
Figure 9.1:	The Proscenium Stage	86
Figure 9.2:	The Proscenium Stage Positions	87
Figure 9.3:	Horizontal Movements	89
Figure 9.4:	Curved Movements	89
Figure 9.5:	Vertical Movements	90
Figure 9.6:	Diagonal Crossing Movements	90
Figure 9.7:	Angular Movements	91
Figure 10.1:	The Thrust Stage	93
Figure 11.1:	The Traverse Stage	97
Figure 12.1:	Ekuechi Facekuerade Performance stage	104
Figure 12.2:	Procession and Staging of Ekuechi Facekuerade Performance	109
Figure 13.1:	Stage Areas	112
Figure 13.2:	Charts Showing Strengths of Movements	113

Figure 13.3:   Theatre Body Positions   115
Figure 13.4:   Theatre Blocking Positions   116
Figure 13.5:   Blocking Positions   117

Foreword

In about March 2016, I got a call from someone who introduced himself as Tekena Mark of the Department of Theatre Arts, University of Port Harcourt. He said he had read some of my publications and had become my follower before he met one of my undergraduate ex-students, Mrs. (now Dr.) Lillian Mokwunye, his fellow postgraduate student at the University of Port Harcourt, from whom he obtained my phone number. He said he had completed the manuscript of a book, *Directing the Play*, and would be grateful if I could write its foreword. "What has this young lecturer learnt about or done in theatre directing that he wants to publish *Directing the Play*? I mused. My bias – if you might call it that - stemmed from my experience of a number of books from those who are in a hurry to be called authors, which I picked up from learned/professional conferences and found errors of content and expression from their very first paragraphs. However, out of sheer curiosity, I asked my caller to send his manuscript to my email, but I warned that I had so many irons in the queue in my fire and needed time to work to his. I also warned that I do not write a foreword until I was sure that the work of which I was writing it was of high quality. Young Tekena was not daunted. He boldly sent his manuscript! Several months after, it was time to deal with Tekena's manuscript. In an attempt to flip through it to find easy faults, I got firmly gripped by the rich content and excellent presentation of the work. I returned to the first page and began to study!

After my first study of the manuscript, my real dialogue with Tekena began; I found that he had not only majored in Directing for his bachelor's and master's degrees and, consequently, directed plays at those levels but has since been researching and teaching Directing. I found that he was also on a PhD programme, studying two Nigerian directors. (He has now obtained the PhD.) Finally, I found he was a perfectionist, spurred by every well-reasoned comment to revise and push his work towards perfection. Consequently, what began as a manuscript of nine chapters, after three thorough-going and largely self-motivated revisions, ended up as a manuscript with fourteen chapters! I have no doubt that if this manuscript was left in his hands, this young perfectionist would keep transforming it. But he should save his energy for issuing a revised edition in future if he finds that necessary. Right now, the theatre world can no longer wait for this fresh, well-researched, well-articulated, pioneering work, which is a historical survey, a theoretical study and a directing manual.

As I hinted earlier, *Directing the Play* has fourteen chapters. Chapter One contains a robust introduction and, among other things, enunciates the general objective of the book, which is "to provide a complete guide on how directors can interpret plays on the arena, proscenium, thrust, traverse and the traditional African theatre stages". To equip its readers to do this, the book, in its other thirteen chapters, executes a number of specific objectives. Chapter Two deals with the Director in Theatre History – how directing began and has developed, types, qualities, functions of the director and his tools. Chapter Three considers the principles of directing – composition, picturization, movement, rhythm, and pantomimic dramatization. In Chapter Four, apart from studying the theories of long-researched and copiously documented largely Western directors, the book breaks new ground in Chapter Five as it also examines the directing techniques and work of well-known but not so well-documented Nigerian and Ghanaian directors. Chapter Four begins with the "Pictorial Motion and Ensemble Playing" technique of George II, Duke of Saxe-Meiningen, and "The System" of Constantin Stanislavski and proceeds to the "Poor Theatre" of Jerzy Grotowski. Chapter Five examines Ola Rotimi's technique of the "Pressure Cooker, Festival Theatre and Convoluting Concourse of Variegated Happenings", then it widens its focus to include Sam Ukala and his "Folkism" technique, Dapo Adelugba and his "Dauduism or Adelugbaresque" technique; Henry Leopold Bell-Gam and his "Aquatic Theatre" technique; Effiong Johnson and his "Impact-Contact Aesthetics" technique; the "Neo-Alienation Aesthetics" technique of Abdul Rasheed Abiodun Adeoye; the "Facekuerade Theatre" technique of Sunday Enessi Ododo; "Cosmo-Humo Symbiosis" technique of Inih Akpan Ebong and the "Anansegoro" Technique of Efua Theodora Sutherland. In this chapter, the book achieves the great feat of having all these directors studied in one space. One may wonder why a number of other important Nigerian directors, such as Wale Ogunyemi, Femi Osofisan, Zulu Sofola, Bode Sowande, Wole Soyinka, Kalu Uka, etcetera, are not studied here. Could it be because these directors did not formulate theories for their practice or because they have been sufficiently studied?

Chapter Six delves into the directing techniques of directors from South Africa, North Africa, and East Africa. It begins with the "Workshop and Physical Theatre" technique of the South African director, Bheki Mkhwane, then moves on to the "Poetics of Confrontation" technique of the Tunisian director, Fadhel Jaibi, and finally to the "Improvisational Directing" technique of the Kenyan director, Joseph Murungu.

In Chapter Seven, the book studies the development of the Western theatre stage from the Classical period through the Middle Ages, Renaissance England, and the Restoration Period to modern times before focusing on the development of the African traditional theatre stage. Chapters Eight, Nine, Ten, Eleven and Twelve identify and explain the characteristics, advantages, disadvantages, and directorial implications of directing on the arena stage, proscenium stage, thrust stage, traverse stage and African traditional theatre stage, respectively. Chapter Thirteen may be read as a theoretical exposition or a manual of the crux of directing, blocking and movement. It deals with characters' movement and physical behaviour, stage orientations and emphasis, body positions, blocking positions, acknowledgement and support, and implementing choices. It also distinguishes between blocking for the stage and blocking for the screen. In Chapter Fourteen, the final chapter, the author explains directorial concept and directorial approach, which many external examiners quiz final year directing students on.

Directing the Play is a bold and pioneering work, well-illustrated with sketches, figures, and plates. It is the product of the rich experience of a precocious author hungry to contribute to the development of his profession by offering an uncommon text, which would serve as an introductory handbook to neophytes and a quick refresher of old hands. It is a book that everyone interested in the fascinating discipline of Theatre Arts should possess.

Professor Sam Ukala   February 2020

Chapter 1

Introduction

Background to the Study

The word theatre has attracted a lot of meanings over the years. For some, the word theatre means a building, a place or an area where dramatic performances take place. It could mean the performance itself in the presence of a live audience. Theatre can be seen as a discipline; the discipline of Theatre Arts, or a course which people study or undertake to get professional training as theatre artists. According to Cohen (2000, p.7), "the word 'theatre' comes from the Greek word 'theatron', which means the seeing place; a place where something is seen." Theatre can also refer to the plays which a theatre troupe presents. Hence the word theatre can be seen as a building, a troupe (a company of players), and an experience; in which the members of the audience come to witness or experience the performance of plays by actors. In this sense, theatre refers to the combination of people, ideas and the works of art that are produced from this combination.

Theatre as a collaborative art requires certain basic elements before it can take place. These elements are the story, the performers, the space and the spectators. The story is the idea which may be scripted or improvised. The performers are the actors that perform the dramatic actions. The space refers to the stage or place where the performance takes place, while the spectators are the members of the audience who view the dramatic actions. Most theatre performances require the collaboration of many theatre personnel such as the playwright, director, actors, designers, technicians, composers, instrumentalists, singers, choreographers and dancers, and all production components (script, actors, scenery, costumes, lighting, music and dance) which must be knitted together skillfully in order to produce a unified aesthetically pleasing impression before the audience.

Ejiofor (2007, p. 4) holds that "theatre and drama actually began with the earliest man's antics at imitating animals around campfires, in a bid to increase his hunting game and ensure survival in what has come down to us today as sympathetic magic." And in the course of this game, he developed a form of undisguised imitation of his environment where he performed dances, sang, made music, and even used masks in rituals. From the foregoing, theatre can be said to have originated from the ritualistic practices of man. Later, as development ensued, these rituals began to lose their religious significance and roles, taking on secular functions.

Theatre has served a number of functions; first, it served as a form of religious activity, especially during the classical era, when the Greeks employed theatre in their worship of Dionysus, the Greek god of wine and fertility. Theatre, as a performance, has been used for education, information and entertainment. According to Robert Cohen (2000, p. 21), "theatre is a performance which entails a series of actions by actors for the ultimate benefit of the audience." For Eric Bentley, "all the many definitions of theatre can be reduced to: A performs B for C" (cited in Brockett and Ball, 2013, p. 6). This entails that someone performs something for someone else. He identifies three basic elements of theatre; these are: "what is performed (a play, scenario or plan), the performance (including all the processes involved in the creation and presentation of a production), and the audience" (the perceivers) (cited in Brockett and Ball, 2013, p. 6). This, therefore, means that for theatre to exist, these three basic elements must be present. In the same vein, the whole process of creatively interpreting a play or performance before an audience at a particular place and time is known as 'directing', and the person who handles this function in the theatre is known as the director.

Concept of Directing

Directing is the staging of a play's abstract world before a live audience. According to Jacques Copeau, a nineteenth-century French theatre director, directing is the sum of the creative and technical procedures that enable the play as envisioned by the author to move from an abstract, latent state (that of the written script) to concrete and actual life on stage. He goes on to say that the more flexible the stage directions are in a script, the more discretion there is for directing, all with the goal of achieving immediate effects (cited in Cole and Chinoy, 1963, p. 214). Another French director regarded as the father of modern mise en scene, Andre Antoine, claims that directing entails the ability to grasp clearly the author's idea in a manuscript, to explain it patiently and accurately to the hesitant actors, and to see the play develop and take shape. To supervise the production down to the smallest detail...To position and train the actors and crew members and harmonize their efforts, and let the work appear in front of so many people (cited in Cole and Chinoy, 1963, p. 90).

Robert Wills (1976, p. 3) defines directing as "the process of transforming personal vision into public performance." This, therefore, means that the director tries to convert his personal vision into reality before an audience using the human and material resources of the theatre. Johnson (2003) agrees with this position when he observes that "directing is an intellectually-tasking, creative theatrical stage activity, which involves the management of artistic personnel and creative devices of the theatre towards a deliberate moulding of a perceived vision, into its most sublime form" (p. 57). Bell-Gam (2007) describes directing as "the auditory or visual interpretation of a play-script by the artistic director" (p. 71). For Oga, it is "the art of harmonizing the contributions of the various artistic collaborators in a theatrical production" (2007, p. 88). Therefore, theatre directing involves the creative interpretation of a play-script by an artistic director using the artistic and non-artistic personnel of the theatre to present a play in the presence of an audience at a given place and at a particular time.

Aim and Objectives of the Study

The aim of this study is to provide a complete guide on how directors can interpret plays on the arena, proscenium, thrust, traverse and African traditional theatre stage orientations. In realizing this aim, this study has set out the following objectives:

1. To examine the concepts of theatre and directing.

2. To examine the work of the director in relation to his workspace – types of stage or performance area - and associates – playwrights, actors, designers, etc.

3. To examine some key Western and African theories/techniques of directing.

4. To examine the concepts of movement and blocking and their implications for directors.

5. To examine the meaning of the directorial concept and directorial approach and their implications for directors.

Rationale for the Study

From the classical era to the modern era, a sizable number of books on the art of directing have been written. Many of these books have concentrated on different facets of the discipline of directing, covering topics like the definition, history, and development of directing as well as the qualities, roles, and types of directors. However, major areas of directing that have not received much scholarly attention include works that serve as guides for aspiring directors and studies that reflect the theory and practice of directing in Africa and examine the characteristics, advantages and disadvantages and the implications of directing on the arena stage, the proscenium stage, the thrust stage, the traverse stage, and the African traditional theatre stage. This book attempts to fill these gaps as well as make the art of directing easier for practising and aspiring theatre directors. This monograph was developed from my lecture notes and intended to address the challenges practising or would-be directors face. The author did not receive any funding for this research.

Significance of the Study

This book will be of immense benefit to budding and established directors, students and teachers of theatre and drama departments in schools and universities. The need for the book arises from the fact that most books on play directing focus on Western directors, ignoring the contributions of African theatre practitioners. While studies on directing, such as Weinstein (2012), Dean and Carra (2009), and Johnson (2003), provide insights on the art of directing from a general perspective, Emasealu (2010) and Uwatt (2004) document the directorial practice of the Nigerian director, Ola Rotimi. However, this book's advantage over existing works is that it documents Ola Rotimi's directorial style along with the performance theories of Western and other African directors and examines the directorial implications of the Arena, Proscenium, Thrust, Traverse, and the African Traditional Theatre Stage orientations. It would therefore serve as a contribution to the body of works on the art of directing and a valuable work book for directors and theatre practitioners in general

Research Method

This study employed the archival, interview, and descriptive research approaches of the qualitative research method to realize set aim and objectives. It relied on primary and secondary sources to gather the data for this research. The primary sources of data included interviews with directors/theorists on directing and the researcher's years of experience as a theatre practitioner, while the secondary sources of data were relevant text books, journal articles, the internet, etc.

Definition of Operational Terms

For the purpose of clarity, let us define some key terms as they have been used in this study. These are theatre, directing, director, stage, theory, blocking, movement, concept and approach:

Theatre: In this study, theatre means a building or space where an audience sees performances and the performances themselves.
Directing: This is the artistic and creative interpretation of a play by an artistic director before an audience at a specific place and time.
Director: This is the theatre personnel who is responsible for interpreting plays on stage.
Stage: This is the place where a dramatic action is reenacted.

Theory: This is a principle derived through experiments that governs the practice of an art, usually propounded by an authority in the (field of) art.

Blocking: This is a director's movement of an actor from one stage area to another.

Movement: This is the displacement of the body of an actor from one stage area to another in relation to other actors, set properties and the stage space.

Concept: This is an idea or notion of a thing or phenomenon.

Approach: This is a particular perspective from which an action is executed, especially from which a play is directed on stage.

Chapter 2

History, Qualities, Tools, Types and Functions of the Director

Development of Directing

The recognition of the director as an independent artist occurred less than a century ago. According to Clurman (1972), "the director as we know him today is a product of the nineteenth-century theatre," and "modern directing began in 1866 with the Duke of Saxe- Meiningen" (p.9), and the development of directing has had much to do with the development of modern theatre which has witnessed a lot of dramatic innovations. This gradual process of the evolution of theatre directing will be examined under four phases, which are: Phase One -Teacher Directors, Phase Two - Realistic Directors, Phase Three - Stylizing Directors, and Phase Four - Contemporary Directors.

At the very beginning of theatre, in classical Greek and Roman times, directing was seen as a form of teaching. Playwrights often directed their own plays. The Greeks referred to the director as 'Didaskalos', which meant teacher. In the Middle Ages, medieval religious plays had an individual or group of individuals who directed them; and the director was designated as 'Master'; a teacher. Cohen (2000) claims that the fundamental tenet of teaching is that the teacher already knows and comprehends the material; the teacher's job is to merely convey that knowledge to others. The 'master of the secrets or machines' was in charge of ensuring the creation of realistic effects, and the actors (most of whom were amateurs) reportedly worked out their own blocking and business, with the exception of situations where specific motions, movements, or stage positions had already become customary or when professional minstrels were employed to play significant roles (Pickering, 1981).

Cohen (2000) observes that by the eighteenth and nineteenth centuries, because of the discovery of science, an age dedicated to rationalism fostered a profusion of libraries, museums, and historic preservation, which emphasized accuracy, consistency and precision in the arts. There were major directorial changes in the theatre because audiences were now demanding the revival of classical plays whose authors were no longer alive to direct them and that this revival be historically edifying, and that they have museum-like authenticity (p. 457). This required research and some form of coordination and organization; hence, it demanded an independent director. Cohen further records that no director was recognized or received credit for their efforts. Sometimes the credit would go to a famous acting star such as the Englishman Charles Kean or the American Edwin Booth, when in the real sense; the work was done by a lesser functionary. Nevertheless, these teacher-directors who laboured tirelessly began the art of directing as we know it today. They organized their productions around specific concepts and dedicated themselves to creating unified and coherent theatrical works by directing an ensemble of actors, designers, and technicians towards established ends (2000, p. 457).

The second stage of the development of modern directing started by the end of the nineteenth century and brought with it a group of directors who reexamined old theatrical conventions and looked for ways to make theatrical productions more lifelike. George II, the Duke of Saxe-Meiningen, was the first in this group and is regarded as the first modern director. Cole and Chinoy comment that May 1, 1874 has come to occupy a special position in the history of the director because on that date, the Duke of Saxe-Meiningen sent his unknown troupe to Berlin to exhibit the exceptional accomplishments of a director's theatre. To create genuine stage representations, the Duke of Saxe-Meiningen used innovations...intensive rehearsals, discipline, integrated acting, and historically accurate sets and costumes. But the Duke went far beyond his predecessors in attempting to reconcile the normally seductive illusions of the painted set with the moving actor...He translated the text using all of the theatrical arts... He combined the visual and aural arts to create a "symphony of visual and aural minutiae" (cited in Johnson, 2003, pp. 54-55).

As a result, the Duke presided over his team of Meiningen actors and assumed the role of director, having exclusive responsibility for assembling, leading, and guiding the complete production team in the direction of a predetermined objective. The Meiningen Company's influence was felt throughout all of Europe, and even after the company stopped touring in 1890, the role of a director who organized and prepared an entire cast for a complex and thorough theatrical presentation had already become well-established (Cohen, 2000, p. 458).

Taking the lead from the Duke's approach to theatrical productions, Andre Antoine in France, and Constantin Stanislavski in Russia, adjusted their directing styles in semblance of that of the Duke. Cohen notes that Constantin Stanislavski started his work with his Moscow Art Theatre in 1898, while Andre Antoine started a drive toward more realism in Paris in 1887 with his Theatre Libre. Based on the Duke's staging approach, both directors created original acting and actor-training methods. Both theorized and worked pragmatically at the organizing of theatre companies, the development of a dramatic repertory, the re-education of theatre-going audiences, and the recreation of the overall aesthetics of the theatre (2000, p. 485). As naturalists, these two directors strove to make the theatre a powerful social and artistic instrument for the expression of truth and expanded the directorial function into an all-encompassing art. The rise of realism in the nineteenth and early twentieth centuries and the rise of directors who strove to make productions more realistic and highly theatrical opened the way for the irresistible innovations that established the importance of the director. Other directors in this category include Harley Granville-Barker in England, David Belasco in America, and Otto Brahm in Germany.

The third phase was one that ushered the director to the position of power and authority as we know him today. "This phase arrived with directors who joined forces with non-realistic playwrights to create the modern anti-realistic theatre" (Cohen, 2000, p. 458). These directors demanded that the theatre director should aim primarily at the creation of originality, theatricality, and style in theatre productions. These directors believed that truth was beyond reality and, for the director to create a truthful theatre; he must go beyond the confines of reality. They did not keep to the rules of verisimilitude; their goal was to produce sheer theatrical brilliance, beauty and excitement and to lead their collaborators in explorations of pure theatre and pure theatrical imagination (Cohen, 2000, p. 459).

Paul Fort was one of the first of this group of directors to launch his Theatre d' Art in 1890 in Paris, which was a direct assault on the realistic principles of Andre Antoine. In the same vein, Vsevolod Meyerhold, a one-time disciple of Stanislavski, began his theatre of biomechanical constructivism. Meyerhold produced several symbolic plays in Moscow theatre, according to Lawal (2010, p.40). He rejected Stanislavski's realism and started to develop his own theory of symbolism, sometimes known as conditional theatre, which calls for physical stretching. In accordance with Gordon Craig's vision, he produced a number of surrealistic plays in which the players were treated as manipulable puppets. Meyerhold's theatre, according to Cohen, comprised an acting approach typified by bold gestures and quick, near-acrobatic movement. The drive toward a stylized type of directing introduced lyricism and symbolism, as well as an explosive theatricality and some purposefully constructed methods of performing, which has had a tremendous effect on modern theatre and drama (2000, p. 459).

The most important and influential figure in this phase is a man, who is not himself a director, but a stage designer and theorist, named Gordon Craig. In his essay titled "The Art of the Theatre" (1905), Craig compared the director of a play to the captain of a ship, an absolutely indispensable leader whose rule, maintained by strict discipline, extends over every last facet of the enterprise (Cohen, 2000, p. 459). For him, "until discipline is understood in a theatre to be willing and reliant obedience to the director or captain, no supreme achievement would be accomplished" in the theatre (Cohen, 2000, p. 459). Craig aimed at a full renaissance of all the arts of the theatre in which a systematic progression of transformation would overtake all the arts: acting, scenery, costuming, lighting, carpentering, singing, dancing etc., under the complete control and organization of the independent director.

Having gone through the three successive phases of development of directing, today we are in the fourth phase, which is the 'Age of the Contemporary Director', an age where the directorial functions have been firmly established as the "art of synthesizing script, design, and performance into a unique and splendid theatrical event that creates its own harmony and its own ineffable yet memorable distinction" (Cohen, 2000, p. 460). The director is himself a unifier of the various contributions of other theatre collaborators in order to create a memorable experience on stage before an audience and to communicate by the simultaneity of sensory impressions.

In a world of increasing complexities as a result of man's attempt to capture space and adapt to the constantly changing environmental and socio-cultural conditions, man is constantly in search of better and newer ways of overcoming the seeming challenges created by his activities or by nature. The theatre artist and, indeed, the director is not left out; he, too, is looking for better ways of creating a scintillating and fresh theatre experience. In today's theatre, the director is constantly faced with the challenges of trying to satisfy, and please the audience and this is borne out of the fact that all too often, in today's world, "the exotic quickly becomes familiar and the familiar just quickly becomes trite or overused" (Cohen, 2000, p. 460).

Consequently, there are hardly any rules for the director; nothing is binding because his function has graduated from just teaching what is ideal to creating productions that are captivating and stimulating. A director today has a lot of options before him when doing a production, he can decide to borrow from the theatrical conventions of the past, of the present, or he could decide to project into the future in a sort of experimental journey, with a view to creating higher realities through stage pictures. Our conglomerate theatre of today, as Cohen puts it, "allows Shakespeare in modern dress, Greek tragedy with a kabuki spectacle, theatre of the absurd as vaudevillian buffoonery, and romantic melodrama as campy satire" (2000, p. 460). Hence, in today's theatre, no style is obligatory, no interpretation is final, and no question can be answered with finality. The modern director and theatre are condemned to be free, and the director's freedom in the face of limitless possibilities is challenging and thrilling. According to SU, a Nigerian director, this phase also embraces directors whom Albright et al. (1968, p. 448) call "ruthless adapters", directors who take the script as a launch pad for the expression of their own personal ideas, who take the script as a point of divergence, who see themselves as the be-all-and-end-all in the theatre and subject everyone – playwright, actor, designer – to their own authority, interpreting their own minds rather than the playwright's, the likes of Peter Brook and many others (SU 2017, personal communication, 21 January).

Qualities of the Director

The director, according to Clurman (1972, p. 14), must be an organizer, a teacher, a politician, a psychological investigator, a lay analyst, a technician, and a creative entity. Ideally, he should be familiar with literature (drama), acting, acting psychology, visual arts, music, history, and, most importantly, people. He must inspire trust, which means he must be an excellent lover. More so, a director must be logical when making decisions and not rely on sentiments because sentiments could hamper production. The director must learn to have a warm disposition towards those he is working with. He must be disciplined, regular, time conscious and punctual at rehearsals. He must have good listening and observing abilities. He must be humble.

According to Oga (2007), one of the most noticeable attributes of a competent director is humility. It is crucial to highlight, however, that such humility should not be confused with stupidity. At appropriate times, he may welcome suggestions, comments, and thoughts. However, the director should never allow actors or other theatre employees to take over his role (p. 90). A director must have high cognitive and intuitive abilities; he must be intelligent. He must be diplomatic, imaginative and creative. He must possess managerial skills. He must know how to manage the human and material resources of the theatre. He must learn and know how to manage time; he must be patient, accommodating, and also authoritative. He must be knowledgeable in the arts, familiar with play productions, willing to learn, ready to accept challenges and confident in himself. He must be good in public relations and must possess the sixth sense.

The Director's Tools

The sole duty of the artistic director is to interpret the script creatively in collaboration with other artists in the theatre's three-dimensional space, giving shape, sound, rhythm, images and unity to his artistic vision in the presence of an audience. In doing this, the director works with three basic tools: the actors, the script, the space or stage and other artistic collaborators like the lighting designer, set designer, costume designer etc. The actors are the human personnel who embody the roles in the play. They are the agents of the action. They assume the roles created by the playwright by suppressing or augmenting aspects of their personality in order to reveal the actions and motivations of the characters in a play at a particular point in time. The director cannot do without them. The script is the raw material with which the director builds his interpretation. It provides him with the idea or story. The script may be written, as in a playtext or unwritten, where the director relies on improvised storylines and works this out with actors to create theatre. The script serves to guide the director as he performs his creative and interpretative functions.

The space or stage is the place where the performance takes place. Wherever is found suitable for locating the drama is the space or stage. It may not necessarily be a raised platform. The space is the venue for the performance; it is where the director works with the actors, the place where the dramatic action is carried out. A director needs a space to enable him to function and actualize his objectives, but in addition to these tools, the director also requires time, costumes, make-up, lighting, designs and adequate funding to realize his goals.

According to Bell-Gam (2007), an artistic director should budget appropriately for the production because he does not work alone but in partnership with other theatre professionals (p. 73). The director's interaction with the designers is that he organizes meetings with them in which he discusses his vision for the production and harmonizes it with the numerous thoughts and conceptions of the designers regarding the production. He also supervises their operations throughout the play production process.

Types of Directors

Broadly speaking, there are four types of directors, which Oscar Brockett, Cameron and Hoffman, and Edwin Wilson have all identified. The first is referred to as one that faithfully follows the playwright's script to arrive at the playwright's vision (the slavish director). According to Johnson (2003), quoting Cameron and Hoffman, this type of director is a slave because he recognizes, accepts, and obeys the playwright as his master. This type of director is unable to see beyond the script. This is the director who follows all instructions from the playwright and, if he has any reservations, seeks clarification from the playwright (p. 67). The second type of director is the Auteur director, who, according to Johnson (2003), picks up a script and interacts with it meaningfully to the point of using it as the basis for production. This director is still adaptive and independent enough, and in an effort to further the expression of his or her vision, he or she is willing to add to or delete from the text without hesitation (p. 68).

Differentiating the third type of director - the Mild adapter director, from the auteur director, SU opines that the Mild adapter director makes creative amendments to the play in order to enhance the thought and vision of the playwright. The amendments range from changing a few inappropriate words or lines to expunging an unclear or dull section and/or rewriting it. The more essential/elaborate his amendments, the more the director qualifies to be called a "co-author". Young or inexperienced playwrights benefit immensely from the work of such a director. But the "auteur" (French for "author") director assumes authorship, replaces the author, and makes the work essentially his, bearing the indelible and overwhelming inscriptions of his concepts and style; hence Cook describes him as "prime author". He is a ruthless adapter of the original script to the extent that he could make the play communicate the exact opposite of the original author's thoughts (SU 2017, personal communication, January 21, 2017).

Unlike the faithful or "slavish" director who holds the script sacrosanct or the creative interpreter or mild adapter director, who makes amendments to improve the effectiveness of the script and sharpen the playwright's vision, the auteur director is more interested in experimenting with techniques, form and content. The hallmark of auteur directors include:

- They repeatedly return to the same subject matter.
- They habitually address a particular psychological or moral theme.
- They employ a recurring style.
- They stick to a particular genre.
- They demonstrate any combination of the above.

David Cook (2004) describes the auteur-director as "that particular director with a recognizable and distinctive style, who is considered the prime 'author' of a film" or, in this case, a stage production (p. 910).

The fourth type of director, according to Milly Barranger (1991), is the opposite of the auteur-director and serves as the servant or coordinator of a group of actors, de-emphasizing his vision for the play and instead opening up much more to the suggestions, criticisms, and encouragements of the group (p. 94). This kind of director is a team player. According to Barranger, the director and performers collaborate during rehearsals to establish movement, gestures, character interactions, stage pictures, and line readings. Instead of going into the rehearsal stage with predetermined ideas, the director observes, listens, makes suggestions, and makes choices as the performers rehearse the play (1991, p. 98). This style of collaborative approach to directing is common with experimental directors like Bertolt Brecht, Peter Brook, Richard Schechner, Eugene Barbara, Joseph Chackin, Johnny Papp, and so many others.

Functions of the Director

In most professional theatre outfits, the director is assigned a play to direct, while in others, he is often in a position to choose the script himself. The director's job is more artistic than managerial as he interprets the script, casts actors, rehearses them, works with other artistic and non-artistic collaborators in designing a production, and coordinates all elements into a finished production. The artistic functions of the director include script selection, analysis of the script, setting up of a production committee and convening production meetings, auditioning of actors, casting of actors, coaching and rehearsing of actors, and staging the play, while the managerial functions of the director include scheduling of meetings, organizing rehearsals, and liaising with other professionals of the theatre.

The first function a director performs is to determine the choice of script or play based on his interest and the likely interest of his audience. A lot of factors influence his choice of script; Bell-Gam (2007, p. 74) outlines these as the purpose of the play, the number of cast members, the social and cultural relevance of the play, the thematic contents, the budget, the venue of the proposed performance, the dramatic genre, the availability and adaptability of the actors and actresses, the target audience, and the given circumstances (the geographical location which includes climate, date, year, season, time of the proposed production, economic environment, political environment, and the religious environment of the play).

After determining the script, the director analyzes the script to enable him to develop ways of staging the play. But this depends on his point of view about directing, which will enable him to develop a "master metaphor" or "directorial concept" for the production. Harold Clurman refers to this as the spine, the main action or the general action that motivates the play, while Stanislavski calls it the super objective. According to Trumbull (2008), Cameron and Gillespie outlined two approaches to the analysis and interpretation of script by the artistic director; the first is the Worshipful approach. Here the director's job "is not to create theatre, but to cause the script or play to create exciting theatre. The director depends solely on the playwright's concept when analyzing the script." The second is the Heretical approach, where the director's job "is to interpret the text in order to make a theatrical entity of the entire production for the audience. The director's responsibility is to unite all arts of the theatre into an artistic whole, of which the script is only a part" (Trumbull, 2008). Analysis of the script also helps the director determine the play's structure, the tone and impact or intended effects of the play, the highs and lows of the play, and how to give theatrical excitement to each.

The next function the director performs is that he constitutes a production committee and holds production meetings to discuss, develop concepts, and get these ideas across to other artistic collaborators without restricting interpretations. Hal Prince, a very famous director and producer, once said, "the worst thing that can happen is to get back from artists exactly what you ask for" (Trumbull, 2008). After setting up a production committee, the director conducts an audition, where he does a practical examination of interested artists for a production to enable him to determine their suitability for roles in a play. He, therefore, subjects them to a practical demonstration of their talents. Once the audition has been conducted, the director casts actors or assigns roles to those who were successful during the audition. For Bell-Gam (2007), this process should be carried out as honestly as possible, with no sentiments and without the use of friendship or ethnicity as criteria for casting. The play's required characters should only be played by actors who are the best fit (p. 76).

When casting, the director considers the actor's theatrical background, the actor's creative ingenuity and sensitivity, the actor's imaginative potential, the actor's acting experience, the stage presence and personality of the actor before the audience, the actor's personal and emotional dispositions in relation to the character in view, the actor's ability to handle the proposed character in the play, the actor's voice and eloquence and the actor's physical, mental and health dispositions (Bell-Gam, 2007, p. 76). After casting, the director rehearses the actors; trains and guides them so that they will become conversant with their parts. Rehearsals are tryouts or practices to enable actors to become acquainted with their roles and the dramatic actions in the play. Stanislavski's influence has led to collaboration between directors and actors. The director, therefore, advises, inspires, encourages and helps the actors see other dimensions in the production as well as in knowing their parts.

When preparing a play for public performance, the director schedules five types of rehearsals: readthroughs, blocking rehearsals, polishing rehearsals, technical rehearsals, and dress rehearsals. According to Vaux (2017), rehearsals often last six to eight weeks and allow the cast to master their lines, develop their movements, and discover the emotional core of the piece. During rehearsals, the director directs the cast to ensure that all of the actors and technical parts of the production (lights, sound, and sets) blend into a united and consistent whole.

Vaux (2017) asserts that read-throughs often occur one or two times at the start of the rehearsal phase. At this point, the cast and the director, gather around a table to go over the entire script. Members of the cast read their lines aloud. Before beginning actual rehearsals, read-throughs allow the cast to ask basic questions and get to know one another while also assisting everyone in getting a sense of the play's overall flow and providing the director with the chance to explain how his concepts will be realized on stage. Actors begin to shape the play scene by scene during blocking rehearsals. With the director's help, they iron out the overall shape of the movements and start to understand the play's emotional undertones. Blocking rehearsals typically feature actors dressed casually, general lighting, and a simple set. The director refines and perfects the play's general flow during rehearsals. While the director adjusts the play's pace and tempo and everyone focuses on the play's subtler moments, actors begin to perfect the delivery of their lines and their physical motions. Typically, technical rehearsals last two to three days. The technical aspects of the production, such as lighting placement and cues, precise set changes, and sound cues, are the main focus of these rehearsals. Dress rehearsals, which take place a few days before the major performance, feature actors in full costume and makeup. These practices aim to replicate the performance. In order to give the performers a sense of performing in front of an actual crowd, invited guests occasionally attend, as well as reviewers who may use such rehearsals as the basis for their reviews.

Trumbull (2008) notes that for Cameron and Gillespie, the director-actor relationship can take the following forms during rehearsals, especially blocking and polishing rehearsals: the director as a Parent (authoritarian), as a Guru (visionary), as a Therapist (trust me), as a Seducer (emotional attachment), as a Victim (cajoler), as a Playground Director (let's grow, little planning), as a Lump (vague), and as an Amalgam of the above (probably the best); with preparation and adaptability very necessary, and less actor coaching as performance approaches. The director helps to determine focus, which is the arrangement of the stage picture so as to direct the audience's attention to the appropriate character, object or event. He blocks the actors by determining their movements on stage and their relationship with themselves, the stage properties and the stage space. Furthermore, the director blocks the actors by giving special consideration to stage positions and body positions. He also determines the required stage business actors need and shows actors the best ways to handle props. He determines the visual composition and picturization of the play. He pays attention to movement and shows actors how mood and rhythm can be conveyed through movement. He also determines the play's progression (the rate at which things happen in the play; the speed or the emotional intensity and energy of the dramatic action). After rehearsals must have been completed, the next function of the director is to stage the play, which is the final presentation of the play before a live audience based on the production design. This is after all rehearsals and technicalities relating to the production must have been perfected.

The director also performs managerial functions, one of which is the scheduling of meetings with other theatre collaborators. He schedules meetings with the costume designers, the makeup artist, the lighting designer, and the technical manager. He schedules meetings with the entire production team to discuss ideas about the production. The organization of rehearsals is another managerial function which the director performs. He organizes read-throughs, where he and the actors read through the play and discuss the characters and vision of the play. The director organizes general rehearsals and can decide to rehearse in parts, blocking scenes with particular characters, including "French scenes" (entrance or exit of a character) and scenes between curtains or blackouts. The director also organizes run-throughs of scenes, acts or the whole play. He conducts technical rehearsals, dress rehearsals, previews, or even brush-up or polishing rehearsals.

Another managerial function of the director is that he liaises with other professionals of the theatre; since he is working with not just the artistic collaborators but also non-artistic personnel of the theatre, he must establish a good rapport with these personnel. Speaking on this, Johnson (2003, pp. 80-81) notes that theatre is a composite art that always combines all theatrical components for effect. Establishing a good rapport with other theatre professionals is a must if the director wants the best contributions to the production's success.

Chapter 3

Principles of Directing

The governing principles of directing are the codes and laws that regulate the craft of play directing. They can also be referred to as the basic components of play directing, as defined by Alexander Dean and Lawrence Carra (2009) in the book *Fundamentals of Play Directing*, and are essential components of every well-directed play. Visual and aural aesthetics are the two subcategories of directing codes. According to Dean and Carra (2009), composition, picturization, movement, rhythm, and pantomimic dramatization are all examples of visual aesthetics, whereas Babalola (2017, p. 445) lists music, song, speech, and oratorical art as examples of aural aesthetics along with sound and effect.

Composition

Composition is merely the arrangement of characters and properties on stage by the director for dramatic effect. Composition, according to Bell-Gam (2007), is the realistic arrangement of actors or objects on stage using emphasis, stability, balance, and sequence to achieve beauty (p. 84). According to Oga (2007), composition is the general organization of a stage picture using both animate and inanimate objects to create the environment for the director's dramatic action (p. 93). Emphasis is the drawing of the audience's attention to a significant stage figure or object. Both Oga (2007) and Bell-Gam (2007) define it as the giving of attention by the director to the most significant character or thing on stage. Emphasis can be created using a variety of techniques, including body (the actor's body position; there are eight body positions in the theatre), level (high level, low level), contrast, and focus, especially when using lighting.

Writing on emphasis, Bell-Gam (2007) identifies the following kinds:

Direct Emphasis: Here, only one important stage figure is emphasized.
Duo Emphasis: Here, two characters or stage figures are given emphasis.
Secondary Emphasis: In this type of emphasis, the most insignificant figure is given the emphasis.
Diversified Emphasis: Here, emphasis is given to several figures at the same time (p. 85).

Balance deals with the equal distribution of stage figures/objects on stage so that no part of the stage is heavier than the other. Stability ensures that the stage picture is firm; it is the element of composition that glues the stage picture to the stage area. While sequence is the tying together of units on stage by space; it deals with how a director is able to unite the different stage objects/properties together by space in the course of his interpretation of a play. The picture below shows the use of composition in the production of Ahmed Yerima's *Hard Ground*, directed by Tekena Gasper Mark on the 21st of July, 2015, in the University of Port Harcourt Arts Theatre, a thrust stage:

Figure 3.1: Use of composition in the production of Ahmed Yerima's *Hard Ground*

Source: Tekena Mark's production of Ahmed Yerima's *Hard Ground* (2015)

Mama is standing centre stage right, interrogating Nimi, seated centre stage right. Inyingifaa is seated centre stage left, while Baba is seated upstage centre. In the stage composition, Nimi and Mama gain emphasis. The placement of Baba (seated) upstage centre, Inyingifaa (seated) centre stage left, and Nimi and Mama at centre stage right balances the stage picture and stabilizes the stage composition, while the sequence is seen in the use of space to tie or unite the different stage figures and objects: Baba is seated on a settee upstage centre. A centre table is placed at centre stage. Inyingifaa is seated centre stage left, while Mama and Nimi are placed centre stage right. Nimi is sitting down while Mama is standing, facing Nimi in a diagonal position (Mark, 2015, p. 63).

Picturization

The goal of picturization is to visually depict the relationships between the actors and set pieces or objects on stage. Oga (2007) opines that picturization depicts the emotional connection between items/characters on stage, whereas composition is the general arrangement of objects on stage (p.93).

The director must be aware of the context of the incidents, the socio-economic status of the characters, and the overall setting of the play. Picturization is the image composition creates on the stage. The picture below shows the stage composition and picturization of Scene two in the production of Ahmed Yerima's *Hard Ground*, directed by Tekena Gasper Mark on the 21st of July, 2015, in the University of Port Harcourt Arts Theatre, a thrust stage:

Figure 3.2: Use of composition in Scene Two

Source: Tekena Mark's production of Ahmed Yerima's *Hard Ground* (2015)

The Niger Delta chiefs have come to thank Nimi for his efforts in fighting for the Niger Delta cause. We see drinks and the people of the Niger Delta in Baba's house. The atmosphere is one of celebration. Chief Alabo gives Nimi a hand shake at centre stage left (both standing in a profile position diagonally). Chief Tonye is seated up stage centre, discussing with Christy, who is seated centre stage left, while the people of the Niger Delta are standing behind the chairs. The stage picture evokes in the audience's minds that the mood is festive.

Movement

Movement is referred to as the displacement of the body of actors from one stage area to another. For Oga (2007), movement can be expressed by walking, jogging, or dancing; it is the act of moving across space within time, from one stage position to another. Actors utilize movement in entrances and exits to communicate the mood of a character, emphasize a character or characters in relation to others, evaluate characters and to propose subtextual meanings (p. 93). The use of movement by a director is also captured in the use of blocking (the direction of the movement of an actor in relation to the stage space by a director). To express the use of blocking and aid the understanding of movement in theatre directing, the following significations are used:

Movement Keys

↑	-	Standing or stand
↓	-	Sitting or Sit
←→	-	Lying
↵	-	Turns Left
↳	-	Turns Right
R	-	Running or Run
PR	-	Profile Right
PL	-	Profile Left
M →	-	Moves or Moving
L ∝M	-	Lines and Movement
FF	-	Full Front
FB	-	Full Back
ENT	-	Enters or Entering
EXT	-	Exits
..F	-	Moves two steps forward
..B	-	Moves two steps backward
↵	-	Kneels or Kneeling
USR	-	Up Stage Right
USL	-	Up Stage Left
USC	-	Up Stage Center
CSR	-	Center Stage Right
CSL	-	Center Stage Left
CS	-	Center Stage
DSR	-	Down Stage Right
DSL	-	Down Stage Left
DSC	-	Down Stage Center

CS^{UR}	-	Center Stage Up Right
CS^{UL}	-	Center Stage Up Left
CS^{DR}	-	Center Stage Down Right
CS^{DL}	-	Center Stage Down Left
USR^{UR}	-	Up Stage Right Up Right
USR^{UL}	-	Up Stage Right Up Left
USR^{DL}	-	Up Stage Right Down Left
USR^{DR}	-	Up Stage Right Down Right
--	-	Moves two steps

The picture below shows the use of blocking in the production of *Hard Ground* to highlight the element movement:

A bit in Scene one showing Mama standing CSR interrogating Nimi (seated CSR) over his involvement with the Don. Inyingifaa is seated CSL, and Baba is seated USC.

Figure 3.3: Use of blocking in the production of Ahmed Yerima's *Hard Ground*

Source: Tekena Mark's production of Ahmed Yerima's *Hard Ground* (2015)

In Scene one, light comes on with the song "fiyeo, fika fiyao" to reveal the sitting room of Baba. The mood is pensive, and the song goes off, as Nimi is dSR FF, Baba↑USC, Inyingifaa is⌐CSL, Mama is⌐USL. Nimi⌐with "Now", L∝M "I shall be labeled a vulture... death USR. He M-L∝M CSR "they should have let me die with my friends for the sake of the land", "huum" L∝M "I smell now dSR... "like they do all vultures. They will track me down L∝M,

CSR^{UL}PR..." a trapped rabbit, M-DSR... "why did they rescue me?" L∝M behind the chair "I should have been allowed...the warriors of the land" CSR.

Mama L∝M "warriors my foot" behind the chair USR...only one child. "And now" L∝M – CSR↑ FF. L∝M "my God", DSR↑ FF..."kill me first"⌐ "Nimi" - L∝M-CSR "which of my sins...↑ answer me! Nimi and M-dSR. Mama follows L∝M "kill me, Nimi" DSR. Baba "woman, control...this matter↓USC. Mama "How else" L∝M "my child turns a monster... have him born again USC FF, L∝M " I should have known...made of stone" DSR. Baba "Woman! Go in... need you," ↓USC. Mama⌐ "I shall not go in" L∝M USC behind the chair "I shall wait and hear... to this family" (Mark, 2015, pp. 63-64).

Movement Formations

The director, in his use of the stage space, can take advantage of so many movement formations, such as:

The Circular Formation: Here, the movement composition takes the shape of a circle.

Figure 3.4: Circular Formation

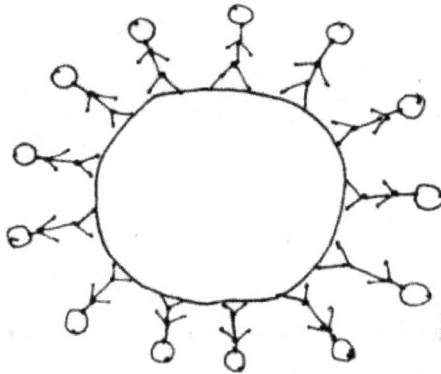

Source: Mark, 2023

The Zig-Zag Formation: The movement composition, in this case, takes the form of a line or course with abrupt alternating right and left turns.

Figure 3.5: Zig-Zag Formation

Source: Mark, 2023

The Serpentine Formation: Here, the movement composition takes the shape of the movement of a serpent or a snake.

Figure 3.6: Serpentine Formation

Source: Mark, 2023

The Straight line Formation: Here, the movement composition is in the form of a straight line, a line without curves or waves.

Figure 3.7: The Straight line Formation

Source: Mark, 2023

The Curve Formation: Here, the movement composition takes the shape of a curved line.

Figure 3.8: Curve Formation

Source: Mark, 2023

The Arc Formation: In the arc formation, the movement composition takes the shape of an arc. An arc refers to a part of a circle or a curve within a circle; it is the circumference of a circle.

Figure 3.9: Arc Formation

Source: Mark, 2023

The Angular Formation: Here, the movement composition takes the shape of an angle.

Figures 3.10 & 3.11: Angular Formations

Source: Mark, 2023

The Square Formation: In the square formation, the movement composition takes the shape of a square.

Figures 3.12 & 3.13: Square Formation

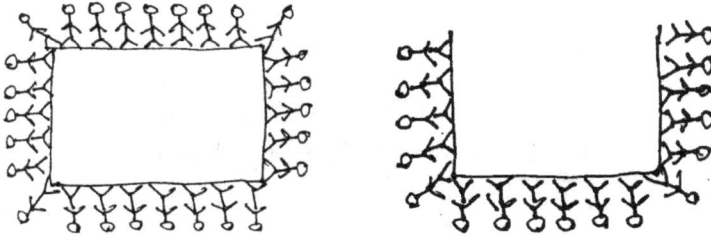

Source: Mark, 2023

The Diagonal Formation: This is a slanted movement formation across the stage that accommodates more people along a line.

Figure 3.14: Diagonal Formation

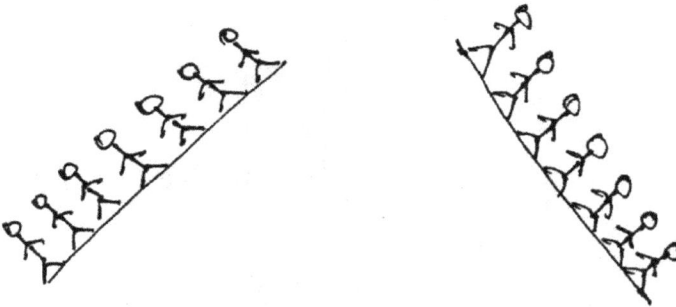

Source: Mark, 2023

Levels, Directions, Dimensions, and Qualities of Movement

Movement can also be appreciated in terms of Levels. Columbus Irisoanga (2000, p. 16) identifies the high, medium, and deep (floor) levels. He submits that "level is an essential element of movement, and to appreciate levels in movement, the body must be bound, lifted or in a jumping position, in motion above the ground" (Irisoanga, 2000, p. 17).

Figure 3.15: Levels of Movement

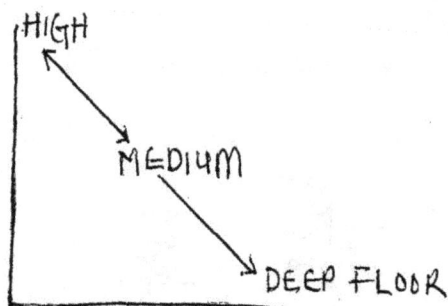

Source: Mark, 2023

Irisoanga (2000, p. 17) also identifies the directions of movement. These are the Right, Left, Forward, and Backward movements. He adds that "if you add the levels of movement to the directions of movement, you will have dimensions of movement: High, Medium, Deep, Right, Left, Forward and Backward" (Irisoanga, 2000, p. 17).

Figure 3.16: Directions of Movement

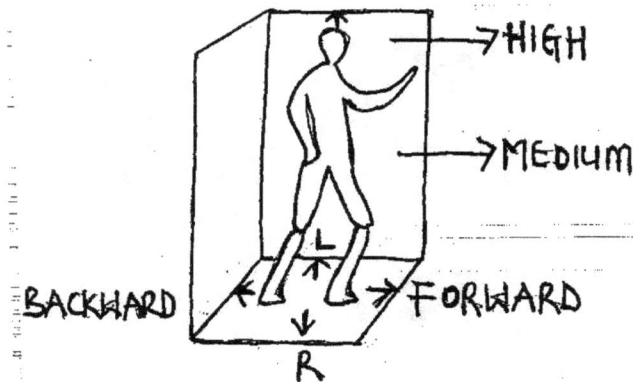

Source: Mark, 2023

Speaking on the qualities of movement, Irisoanga (2000, p. 18) identifies the following as the qualities of movement: Weight/Energy/Force, Space, Time, and Flow.

Weight/Energy/Force: This quality of movement refers to the strength, energy or force of a movement. Energy in this context also implies variation in the intensity of a performance.

Space: This quality of movement deals with how the performers use or move in the general space (periphery space) and the core space (personal space).

Time: Time, in this sense, deals with whether a movement is sudden or sustained; in terms of stimulus.

Flow: This quality of movement can be appreciated in terms of the continuity of a movement or the life of a performance. It can also mean if a movement is free or bound.

Rhythm

Rhythm refers to the response to accented beats. It expresses the vitality and tempo of a play and helps to establish mood, dramatic genre, situation and characterization. It is the movement of the dramatic action from action to action, bit to bit, scene to scene, and from one act to another. Oga (2007) defines it as the ordering of a sequence of aural or visual sensations as perceived by the audience (p. 94). The tempo of tragedy's dramatic action is slower than that of comedy. Rhythm can also be portrayed in a play through the use of songs and music, as well as drums and other rhythm-producing instruments, which help to augment and provide pace to the dramatic action.

Pantomimic Dramatization

Pantomimic dramatization refers to actors' use of gestures, mime, and action without words. According to Bell-Gam (2007), in pantomimic dramatization, meaning is provided to movement and gestures without words or dialogue through actions (p. 84). Pantomimic dramatization is defined by Oga (2007, p. 94) as dramatization that relies heavily on gestures, facial expressions, body language, and movement rather than speech.

Chapter 4

Western Theories of Directing

In the course of the development of the art of directing from its early stages to contemporary times, a number of theatre directors have developed certain directing styles and techniques. These styles, techniques or approaches have not only been associated with them but have also been entrenched as major styles and theories in the discipline of theatre directing. This chapter shall examine the directing theories and styles of some key Western directors/theoreticians.

George II, Duke of Saxe-Meiningen, and His "Pictorial Motion and Ensemble Playing" Technique

George II, the Duke of Saxe-Meiningen (1825-1914), was a German theatre practitioner who formed a resident theatre company made up of amateurs and gave regular performances in Germany. He is referred to as the first modern director because he produced plays that were historically accurate in the nineteenth century. He designed all the costumes, scenery, and properties used by his troupe. He was the first to bring the art of play production into a unified whole. Prior to his time, elements of production were usually separated and relied more on the star actor system. He adopted the practice of long rehearsal schedules and the idea of ensemble playing.

According to Lawal (2010), his rehearsals may run up to five weeks and were used to painstakingly arrange all of the components of a show into a coherent whole. With him came the disappearance of star actors, and as such, all actors were treated equally. As a typical demonstration of this, he acted minor and major roles in his plays (p. 63). He carefully blocked crowd scenes and family groups, making small number of actors seem like a large gathering. He paid a lot of attention to realism (historical accuracy), ensuring that his costumes, set, makeup, properties, music and other production elements captured the period of the play in terms of speech, movement, and action. To reinforce realism in terms of staging, the Duke came up with the idea of stage division. The Duke comments that having a figure in the exact middle of the frame is rarely successful. When feasible, scenery and other items should be positioned on the sides, naturally a given distance from the wings, to be visible to the audience. The actor must always be somewhat to the left or right of the prompter's box rather than exactly in front of him. The actor should only view the area in the middle of the stage, roughly the width of the prompter's box, as a conduit from right to left or vice versa; otherwise, he has no business being there. The same goes for two actors standing in close proximity to the prompter's box. The relationship between the actor and the scenery should also be carefully considered. There must be a valid relationship there (George II, 1963, p. 82).

When it comes to the creation of stage effects by directors, the Duke believes it is critical to keep the middle of the picture from being congruent with the middle of the stage. If the geometric principle of the golden mean is followed, the stage is divided into two even portions, which is likely to result in monotony in the distribution and grouping. Assimilation in the overall picture becomes more or less symmetrical, giving the sense of being wooden, stiff, and dull (George II, 1963, p. 81). He observes that "the charm of Japanese art can be largely attributed to their avoidance of symmetry" (George II, 1963, p. 81). Furthermore, "in graphic arts, the uniformity that the French esthetes call the mother of boredom is symmetry" (George II, 1963, p. 81). The Duke further elaborates, saying that the exception proves the rule; the grouping of the major figure - or the principal mass of figures - in the centre can work out if the adjoining figures or groupings are put on the side at more or less regular intervals. If a strong exalted mood is wanted, it can produce a joyful aesthetic impact (George II, 1963, p. 81). As such, directors in their stage compositions should avoid symmetrical arrangements; rather, their compositions should have variance and be less regular to avoid pictures that appear repetitive and monotonous.

The Duke remarked that combining a live actor with painted scenery is often challenging for directors since every time an actor takes a step back, they appear proportionately larger in relation to the painted settings. The Duke advises actors not to approach a set showing a receding street or any other background perspective so closely that the physical imbalance becomes noticeable. The set elements that the actor must go toward should always be roughly the correct dimensions in respect to the human beings on stage (George II, 1963, p. 82).

The Duke continues by advising actors to avoid leaning on painted scenery (pillars and the like). The stage illusion is destroyed if they move around freely; however, if they move around very carefully so as not to disturb the canvas flat, their stage business conveys a sense of constraint, and they perform in an obviously self-conscious manner. Set items that the actor can sit or lean on, such as doorposts and tree trunks, must be made of durable materials, preferably plastic. In actuality, this is frequently the case in all of our more exclusive modern theatres today. The director should watch out that the diverse materials utilized don't provide two different effects that the audience will find upsetting when both painted, and sculptured items are used on the stage. For instance, transitions from real or synthetic flowers to painted ones must be made with the customary smoothness, making it difficult to tell one from the other (George II, 1963, p. 82).

The Duke advises directors to make sure that actors practice using heavy set pieces, costumes, and accessories as often as possible in order for them to become accustomed to the process of changing these set pieces and donning and taking off costumes (George II, 1963, p. 85). This is especially important when handling crowd scenes with heavy set pieces, costumes, and accessories. The Duke makes the observation that moving from contemporary clothing to historical attire affects movement, particularly carriage and gestures. In older costumes, from the ancient Greek period to the Renaissance, our perfectly familiar way of standing with heels together, which is the accepted one for the military at a halt and which civilians also use to greet superior and notable people, looks out of place and is wholly incorrect (George II, 1963, p. 85). Hence, directors and actors must note that each period in history has costumes and accessories that are peculiar to it, as well as the important manner of movements, gestures and carriage, which actors must be familiar with, especially in plays that require the movement from one historical time to another. The Duke also began the idea of autocratic tradition in the art of theatre directing. Stanislavski copied this tradition but later abandoned it for "The System", which allows actors to use their own imagination rather than depending solely on the director.

Constantin Stanislavski and His "The System" Technique

Constantin Stanislavski (1863-1938) was a wealthy Russian businessman who later became a theatre director. He founded the Moscow Art Theatre and originated the Stanislavki's system of acting, which was spread over the world by his students, such as Michael Chekhov, AlekseiDikip, Stella Adler, Viktor Tourjansky, Richard Boleslawski and others. He started the Moscow Art Theatre as an amateur, together with Vladimir Nemirovich-Danchenko. Both opened the theatre with the staging of *Tsar Feodor* by Aleksei Tolstoy, after which they produced *The Seagull*, written by Anton Chekhov. In 1900, Stanislavski went on tour with the Moscow Art Theatre to Sebastopol and Yalta in Crimea, Russia, where he invited Anton Chekhov to see several productions by his company. Chekhov admired the company's production of his play and respected the theatrical achievements of Stanislavski and Vladimir Nemirovich-Danchenko.

Furthermore, through his own cross-cultural experience as an actor, director, and businessman, he constantly updated his method through inter-disciplinary students, absorbing from a range of sources and influences, such as the modernist and avant-garde developments, Yoga and Pavlovish behaviourist psychology. He introduced group rehearsals and relaxation techniques to achieve better spiritual connections between actors. The Pavlovian approach worked well by conditioning actors through discipline in longer, organized rehearsals and using a thorough analysis of characters. Stanislavski was involved in a long, arduous practice of making every actor better prepared for stage performance and eventually producing a less rigid acting style. He described his early approach as "spiritual realism". His actors worked hard to deliver perfectly believable performances, as none of his actors wanted to hear his famous verdict, "I don't believe".

Lawal observes that "prior to Stanislavski's time, the dominant acting style was imitative and artificial in form, and the height of this was the rhetorical declamation. Based on this, Stanislavski developed an acting theory based on experience than on reason" (2010, p. 36). He observed that "the impediment to natural acting was the actor's state of mind," for him, "the actor's state of mind on stage is unnatural to him because he is acting out what he does not feel inwardly" (Lawal, 2010, p. 36). Finding a way out of this, Stanislavski suggested the idea of the 'Creative State of Mind'; the emphasis here is from the internal to the external, which is a blend of the physical and the psychological. In realizing this, he recommended the following practices and exercises: Freedom and relaxation of the body and the mind, Feeling for truth (this means that the actor must assume the true traits of the character using the principle of the "Magic If"), Functional memory (where the memory that resides in the actor's mind is recalled to the surface of his consciousness by his five senses), Attention (the actor must be attentive in mind and body to other performers in order to make the necessary improvisation especially when he misses a line), Concentration (the actor must forget friends and lovers and put his mind and focus on what is happening on stage), Given Circumstances (these are all the situations in the play which cover scenery, costume, props, place, plot, period and time of action, that should motivate and justify action. The given circumstances complement the magic "If" and enhance the actor's creativity), and the Bits and Pieces (these are the highs and the lows, the climax and anticlimax of each scene, which the actor's interpretation must align with; he or she must be able to communicate the feelings of the character he is representing to his partners and the audience).

The issue with stage communication, in Stanislavski's view, is that it takes place concurrently between the actor and himself, his partner, and the audience. While the actor's contact with their partner is always direct and conscious, the actor's connection with the audience is always unconscious and indirect, and it is always mutual (Lawal, 2010, p. 39). Constantin Stanislavski believes that directors cannot be created, rather, they are born. In his words, "it is possible to create a favourable atmosphere in which he can grow...The true director comprises within his own person a director – teacher, a director – artist, a director – writer, a director – administrator" (Stanislavski, 1963, p. 109).

In discussing the director's function in connection to the actor, he advises that you develop or compose a play to showcase your directorial skills. With enough cleverness, the actor performs with a certain amount of ingenuity, but as long as they don't grasp the meaning of the word "organic," nothing notable will come of it. The differences between theatrical truth and organic truth, as well as between organic and inorganic truths, are no longer widely understood. The query is whether you can have a ready actor with whom I can discuss his part so that he may feel the pressure of my fingers like a piece of clay. Not all clay varieties are appropriate for sculpture, just as not all actors are appropriate for discussions of art. However, if we disregard this first instance, we have to forcefully start everything. The nature of the actor is violated when a director orders an actor, "You must act exactly so." The director's ideas are born out of his own personal memories. Does he need to hear about my sentimental memories? He has his individual. The actor's soul must attract the director like a magnet in order to reveal its contents. To see his worldly side, throw a second magnet after that. The actor's living emotional material is shown in this way by the director (Stanislavski, 1963, p. 110). Theatrical truth, in Stanislavski's sense, means performances that are artificial, spectacular, pompous, and extravagantly histrionic, whereas organic truth refers to performances that emanate naturally from the actors and dramatic situations realistically, as is common in the natural world or everyday life, as such; believability on the part of the audience is not forced but comes naturally.

In response to the question of when he offers his actors the appropriate words, he says he initially tries to give no words at all, focusing only on the action plan. When the actor has mastered that, a particular line of action has grown inside of him, and he starts to feel it with his body and muscles. The actor becomes aware of his destination and motivation at this point. He comes to a point where he has to do something for someone or something. That is a very stressful time. When the actor needs to act verbally, then he supplies the words. At first, they can just act with their ideas, but after he realizes that they understand them and can follow the inner logic and sequence of those thoughts, he tells them to use words. They will then relate to the words differently as a result. They require the words so they can perform them rather than learn them according to their roles. The words are placed not on the tongue muscles or even in the brain but rather in the very soul from whence the actor strives for the super-objective. Then, the words will have a huge impact, having established what are the right deeds and thoughts (Stanislavski, 1963, p. 111).

Stanislavski contends that the director must travel through the entire play until they reach the super-objective while commenting on the need for directors and performers to integrate the pieces of objectives to arrive at the super-objective and to produce a specific action. A most powerful thorough action would result, and the entire role would be largely unconsciously created (Stanislavski, 1963, pp. 112-113). Stanislavski believes that the most powerful tools of the director and actor are the 'through line of action' and the 'super-objective'. For example, "what is our present objective?" Take two-three-four-five cues. You say: "I want to attract attention," and someone else will say, "I try to understand what I am told." The first objective has here been swallowed by the second, and all of them will be swallowed in the end by the super-objective... If you find an actor who adheres fast to the super- objective and follows through action, all the subordinate objectives will be resolved subconsciously (Stanislavski, 1963, p. 115).

According to Moore (1984), when objectives are connected in a logical and cohesive manner, a character's overall course of action is outlined. The idea of the "super-objective" that would support this "through line of action" was created by Stanislavski. The through line of action is the goal that a character has in mind throughout the play that culminates in the super-objective. The objectives could then be viewed as the "vertebrae" and the super-objective as the "spine." For instance, one character's super-objective can be to earn another character's love again. The first character would have subsequent unit objectives such as tease her, satisfy her, thrill her, anger her, and soothe her in order to accomplish this super-objective. When these goals are connected, the super-goal, the rational, cogent course of action, becomes clear. This super-objective is described by Stanislavski as the "ultimate aim of every performance" (pp. 49–50).

In his analysis of the actor's craft, Stanislavski claims that there comes a point when the actor's inner reality and the character come together to cause a certain outcome. Literally, his head is swimming. I'm not sure where I am. Where is the position? And that marks the beginning of the performer and his part coming together. The actor's mood is present, but the role also affects it. The role is innate with the logic of the mood. The circumstances mentioned come from the role. Where the role is and where you are cannot be distinguished. Complete amalgamation has occurred. And at that point, there is unity. The actor positions himself inside the parameters of the role. He needs to develop a distinctive persona. But he continues to be himself. He kills the role if he isolates himself. You deal daily with your feelings. If the emotions are gone, the role is finished. In the picture, you must remain true to yourself. Will I still be the same man if I have a sick leg? If a bee stings me, will I be different? (Stanislavski, 1963, pp. 114–115).

He concludes by saying that the worst mise-en-scène is the one given by the director. In other words, a director may come to a rehearsal with a preset idea of the setting for a production or any other details relating to the production in question, but he should be fluid enough to welcome the opinions of his actors. Performances are more organic if directors welcome suggestions and advice from their actors rather than forcing ideas on them. Later, Stanislavski further improved "The System" with a more physically grounded rehearsal process that came to be known as the "Method of Physical Action". Reducing at-the-table discussions, he now encouraged an 'active analysis' in which the sequence of dramatic situations are improvised and argues that the best analysis of a play is to take action in the given circumstances. His ideas have been used and are still in use by many theatre practitioners, scholars and dramatists such as Micheal Chekhov, Stella Adler, Lee Strasberg etc.

Jerzy Grotowski and His "Poor Theatre" Technique

Jerzy Grotowski (1933-1999) was a Polish theatre director, the founder of the "Theatre Laboratory", and an innovator of the experimental theatre. He also propounded the theory of "Poor theatre". In 1955 he graduated from the High Theatrical School in Krakow with a degree in Acting and proceeded to study Directing at the Lunacharsky Institute of Theatre Arts, where he learnt new trends in theatre pioneered by leading Russian figures such as Stanislavski, Vakhtangov, Meyerhold and Tairov.

According to Justin Cash (2014), Grotowski founded his own theatre company (Laboratorium or the Laboratory Theatre) in 1963, where he and his small group of actors experimented with the physical, spiritual, and ritualistic aspects of theatre, the nature of the role, and the relationship between the actor and the spectator. Grotowski's "Poor theatre" describes a style of performance that does away with the excesses of the theatre, such as lavish costumes and detailed sets, hence the term 'Poor'. Poor theatre focuses on the skill of the actor and is often performed with only a few props. As a director, he preferred to perform works in non-traditional spaces, such as buildings and rooms, instead of real theatre houses or traditional stages. Typically, the audience is placed on many sides of the action or in and amongst the action (Cash, 2014). His acting style places more emphasis on the physical skill of the performer, and actors can transform into other objects. According to Grotowski (1968), "no matter how much theatre expands and exploits its mechanical resources, it will remain technologically inferior to film and television. Consequently, I propose poverty in theatre" (p. 19). He defined "poor theatre" as a theatre whose basic emphasis was on the performer and the audience, not on sets, costumes, lighting, or special effects. These, in his opinion, were only ornaments that, while they might improve the theatrical experience, were not essential to the basic message that the theatre should convey. The word "poor" was used to describe an actor who had been stripped of anything extraneous.

Grotowski jettisoned all costumes and staging, preferring to work with the actor's body. He made his actors go through rigorous training and exercises to enable them to have full control of their bodies. Grotowski was more concerned with what the actor could do with his body and voice without aids, only the visceral experience and the audience. In this regard, he bypassed the traditions of exotic costumes and elaborate staging that had characterized the European theatre prior to his time. This does not mean that he completely avoided the use of lights or sets, but for him, these were secondary and played a complementary role to the already existing excellence the actor could reach with his body. In his book *Towards a Poor Theatre*, he observes that:

> By gradually eliminating whatever proved superfluous, we found that theatre can exist without make-up, without autonomic costume and scenography, without a separate performance area (stage), without lighting and sound effects, etc. It cannot exist without the actor-spectator relationship of perceptual, direct, 'live' communion. This is an ancient theoretical truth, of course, but when rigorously tested in practice it undermines most of our usual ideas about theatre (Grotowski, 1968, p. 19).

Grotowski redefines the theatre, removing all the customary elements of play production, including elaborate lighting, costumes, and scenery, and forcing players and directors to consider the theatre as an act that only requires the actor's body and the audience in order to exist. By being able to function without them, the theatre is not dependent on other production elements. If these elements are there, they must, however, support the actor's artistic vision and not detract from or steal the audience's focus. Thus, Grotowski challenges the idea that theatre is a synthesis of various creative disciplines, including literature, sculpture, painting, architecture, lighting, and acting, under the control of the director. He refers to this "synthetic theatre" as the modern theatre, which he calls the "Rich Theatre" because it is rich in flaws.

Grotowski believes in the sacredness or priesthood of the actor. When the actor enters the sanctity of the performance space, a special event occurs, much like the Catholic Church mass. It is in this space, in the holy relationship between the actor and the audience, that the spectators are challenged to think and be transformed by the theatre. In this sense, Grotowski was one of the key figures in the development of political theatre in the twentieth century. Political and social themes were prevalent in his productions, and his actors relied on their body and voice to bring social transformation to the audience. The theatre is more than just entertainment; the audience serves as its centre and becomes a conduit for learning. Grotowski wanted to present audiences with challenging, upsetting, and experiential theatre; a theatre that places more emphasis on the actor's presence than on image (unlike movies or television).

Chapter 5

West African Directors and
their Techniques

Ola Rotimi and His "Pressure Cooker, Festival Theatre and Convoluting Concourse of Variegated Happenings" Technique

Olawale Gladstone Emmanuel Rotimi (1938-2000) was one of Nigeria's leading playwrights and theatre directors. He has been described as a complete man of the theatre, an actor, director, choreographer and designer who created performance spaces and was influenced by traditional architectural forms. Dapo Adelugba, a Nigerian theatre director and critic, recognizes Ola Rotimi as "one of those theatre practitioners of whom the word on the page takes a secondary place to the work on the stage, and one who places emphasis on the imperative of subjecting his works to the test of rehearsals and performances before publication, to allow for their organic growth as theatrical pieces" (1978, p. 74). Ola Rotimi is the master of the arena stage, and his connection with the audience is direct, tactile, and sensuous, according to Femi Osofisan (1989), who claims that Rotimi has no equivalent on the Nigerian stage when it comes to control of physical space or the manipulation of audience response. Euphonious songs and heartbreaking dirges, poetry rich with echoes of traditional wisdom, colourful costumes, synchronicity of mime and dance gestures, the lure of lights, the dazzle of war spectacle, and the pleasure of ritual are a few examples of the qualities of Rotimi's theatre (cited in Emaselau, 2010, p. 74).

Adelugba contends that "Rotimi's greatest strength as an artist seems to lie in directing" (1978, p. 217), and Yemi Ogunbiyi (1981) argues that "Rotimi's most important contribution to the Nigerian theatre may well not be in the area of playwriting but in the area of real theatre practice." His ability to literally create "magic" on the stage is one of his strongest suits as a theatre practitioner, and his directorial talent may be unrivaled in the country (cited in Emaselu, 2010, p. 75). Emaselu (2010) observes that "Ola Rotimi has been criticized by some and applauded by others for using a penny whistle in the conduct of rehearsals" (p. 119). Another of Ola Rotimi's directorial approaches is the 'Pressure Cooker' technique at rehearsals. The Rotimian pressure cooker technique, according to Emaselu (2010), includes repeatedly and loudly striking idiophonic musical instruments. With this perplexing clangour in the background, the actor must deliver his lines and carry out blockings quickly. This method aids in shortening rehearsal time and makes it possible to quickly recognize the play's entire structural layout (pp. 120–122).

To further accentuate his directing style, Rotimi, in the production note of his play *If: A Tragedy of the Ruled*, describes his intended directorial approach for the play as a "convoluting concourse of variegated happenings", in his words:

> From the viewpoint of directing, this purposefully, is a drama of juxtaposed, variegated actions: a further exploration of theatrical 'naturalness' in the evocation of African atmosphere and rhythms through time, space, sound and matter. Technically here, no action need stop so that another can begins. Sometimes, the actions of one moment crash one upon another, other times they follow one after the other with innate civility, yet 'trippingly-driven in their natural' modes by the tensions of threatened walls (1983, p. viii).

The above is what Abdul Rasheed Abiodun Adeoye (2011) describes as the festival theatre (p. 30). Foluke Ogunyele (2008) records that "the earlier plays that were produced by Ola Rotimi at the Ori Olokun Centre, at the University at Ile-Ife, now Obafemi Awolowo University, reflected the fruits of Rotimi's research" (p. 23). She argues that a university town must necessarily be a polyglot community with residents from many racial and ethnic backgrounds. Rotimi emphasized ethnic harmony as a result, particularly during the Nigerian Civil War. In order to counteract ethnic rivalry, bias, bigotry, paranoia, chauvinism, and extreme states of jingoism, he advocated for inter-ethnic camaraderie or solidarity. He used this to make a call for unity despite cultural differences and to make sure that the audiences could identify with the characters being portrayed onstage (Ogunyele, 2008, p. 23).

Ogunyele (2008) adds that the significant use of local idioms, including music, proverbs, and dances, transformed Rotimi's plays' performances into social gatherings for Yoruba audiences. He wrote about "theatrical apartheid" and how the arch separates the audience from the performances in a very un-African way (Ogunyele, 2008, p.23). Rotimi preferred to direct his plays in the round, as he believed that this reflected the African style for organizing performances. He claimed that his works served two purposes: to correct European historians' misconceptions about Africans and educate our people about ourselves. According to Ogunyele (2008), Rotimi's style was a sympathetic and deliberate pushback against the colonialists' renditions. His writings were centred on the theme of leadership and showed his tragic heroes as admirable leaders who cared for their people (p. 23). A strong point of Rotimi's productions was the use of spectacle. In his words:

You have to address the visuals. The iconography must be clean, clear, gripping, and immediate...arrest the hearing organs of your spectators. The assault must have the same potency visually as the auditory...this is where things like songs instrumentation all come in the rhythm, the power of the spoken word...The visuals...the dynamics of dance, of mimes, gestures, of course the additives of colour, through costumes, makeup, and so (cited in Ogunyele, 2008, p.24).

Also, Rotimi frequently romanced with humour in his works. He is known to introduce humour in his tragedies. He never agreed with critics who frowned at his idea of mixing genres. Rather, Rotimi insisted that he was reflecting an African dimension. His parting words, according to Ogunyele (2008), were: "So I say grab the audience and forget about the critic." He believed that in traditional theatre, the audience is the final arbiter; once they approve of you, to hell with the opinions of others. Rotimi further claims that his intention was to tap into the spectator's emotions in order to get them to think and, if possible, take action (cited in Ogunyele, 2008, p. 24).

Rotimi's achievement as a director is further demonstrated in the World Theatre Festival held in Nancy, France. "The production of *Gbe-ku-de* by Rotimi and the Ori-Olokun players was widely acclaimed by the French reviewers because of Rotimi's adventurous style of production, the enthusiastic devotion of the troupe, Rotimi's mastery of the basic techniques of the theatre and his daring experimentation with new modes of production" (Uwatt, 2002, pp. 9-10). He is also known to shy away from intermission, which he saw as giving the impression of artificiality to the audience. He also did away with curtain calls, which he believes subverts the efforts of creating the illusion of reality necessary for securing empathy. Etherton, M. and Magyer (1981), commenting partly on Rotimi's directorial style, remark that:

Ola Rotimi's plays seem better appreciated for three reasons: His manner of production which emphasizes spectacle: his attempt to involve the audience through the use of the theatre in the round; his avoidance of philosophical abstractions in conception and execution and his language which is without the opulence and sinewy texture of a Soyinka (cited in Uwatt, 2002, p. 10).

He, therefore, proffered through textual and directorial/production techniques a recipe for capturing the Nigerian spectator's interest and then sustaining that interest until it transforms into a state of total empathy, which would give little room for loose talk and catcalls by spectators. Some elements of Rotimi's directorial and managerial virtuosity, as outlined by Kola Oyewo (2000), are "the use of acting areas, repetition, repartee, typecasting, songs and dance movements" (cited in Uwatt, 2002, p. 10).

Other directorial techniques employed by Ola Rotimi are the use of a functional chorus, close performer-audience relationship, emphasis on the actor and the importance of functional speech, the use of indices of traditional African theatre (as seen in the use of songs, dance, music, chant and mime), the use of costume and makeup as expressive arts, the use of set design and lighting as artistic means of communication, the use of stage properties as suggestive arts (suggesting ideas and enhancing the meaning of his productions), the use of sound effects, as well as the use of movement to capture the simultaneity of actions, which is common in the communal nature of the traditional African life. Emasealu (2010) notes that the communal nature of traditional African theatre practice permits concurrent happenings in the open air. Rotimi consistently tries to capture the traditional African use of simultaneous actions in his theatrical presentations to amplify the Africanness of his plays (p. 197).

Rotimi's plays and performances are easy to understand by his audience, and this audience appeal of Rotimi's plays, as observed by Ukala (2000), "derives largely from Rotimi's efficiency at directing the plays rather than their intrinsic qualities" (p. 91). This has made a lot of scholars suggest that he has impacted more as a director than a playwright in the Nigerian theatre. Ukala (2000) notes that if Rotimi is an outstanding director of his own plays, then his plays likely contain excellent seeds that other directors may not have completely recognized or utilized. His use of dramatic experimental language, sharp irony and humour, spectacular excitement, particularly at climaxes, and skilful designs for the use of lights for illumination, scene shifting, and the microphone for surrealistic effects have all contributed to his distinctive style as a director (p. 92).

Rotimi also applies the principles of traditional African performance in his plays, which allows for a good performer-audience rapport and participation in his performances. In this regard, Rotimi declares the paramoucy of the audience in determining the nature of his theatre. In his 'A Charge to the Actors' on the first reading of *Hopes of the Living Dead*, Rotimi makes the observation that 'African audiences think that they too inherently possess acting skills, and are, therefore, in implicit rivalry with the players on stage,' according to Ukala (2000). This brings to mind Ukala's Law 7, or the Law of Ego Projection, which will be discussed later, and it highlights a crucial aspect of traditional African performance: the majority of the audience is familiar with the story, song, dance, or music, and the majority of viewers constantly compare their own abilities with those of the performer, whom they readily correct if he stumbles or commend and collaborate with if he succeeds.

To perform before such an active, critical audience, the actor's primal strategy, Rotimi enjoins, "is to take the initiative. Right from the start of the play. And having taken, sustain it to the end... knowing full well that your ultimate obligation is to your audience" (cited in Ukala, 2000, p. 93). More so, Ukala (2000, p. 93) believes that Rotimi counsels himself in a similar way before he creates a play. His choice of subject and issue, as well as his use of language and sentence structure, show that he is aware of the preferences and tastes of the African audience. As a result, the staging method suggested in his stage instructions closely resembles the traditions of the audience.

Sam Ukala and His "Folkism" Technique

Sam Ukala was a Nigerian playwright, poet, short story writer, actor, theatre director, and film producer. He was a Professor of Theatre Arts and Drama at Delta State University, Abraka, Nigeria. He propounded the theory of "Folkism", the tendency to base literary plays on indigenous history and culture and to compose and perform them in accordance with the aesthetics of African folktale composition and performance. According to Adeoye (2011), Sam Ukala's Folkist style of directing consists of the following components: the use of members of the audience (MOA), a significant amount of accessibility, authenticity, and popularity within Africa, as well as the application of the eight laws of aesthetic response in folktale performance. Directors who seek to use this style should learn and internalize the folkist's icons by studying some of Sam Ukala's plays, such as *Akpakaland, The Slave Wife, Break a Boil, The Log in Your Eye,* etc. (p. 40). This style encourages a good audience-performer relationship.

Ukala makes it clear in his University of Hull, UK, 1994, lecture entitled "Masquerade, Folktale and Literary Theatre of English Expression in Africa" that:

> The African folktale is not prose. It exists only in performance before a live audience. It therefore entails dramatic phraseology, pleasant to speak and to hear; movement, gesture, impersonation, music-making and dancing; and sometimes, costuming, make-up, masking and puppetry (cited in Enita, 2008, p. 50).

Sam Ukala's study of the traditions of performing African folktales served as the impetus for his dramatic aesthetics, which he calls "The Laws of Aesthetic Response" (Godfrey O. Enita, 2008, pp. 50–51). These eight principles were developed as a result of research by J.P. Clark, Efua Sutherland, Ruth Finnegan, and Dan Ben-Amos in various regions of black Africa, which revealed the typical reactions of the narrator and the audience to folktale performances (cited in Enita, 2008, p. 51).

Law 1: The Law of Opening

The opening of an African folktale performance is expected to arouse the audience and to introduce the subject matter and characters of the story. It also offers the audience an opportunity to encourage or stop a prospective performer, depending on the audience's rating as a performer. In Sam Ukala's play *Akpakaland* (1990), the narrator starts the play by leading the audience in the opening song for an Ika folktale performance session. The purpose of involving the audience in the singing and dancing for the opening song is to warm them up and gain their attention; from the very beginning, the audience is invited to participate in the performance (Enita, 2008, p. 51).

Law 2: The Law of Joint Performance

The traditional African audience co-performs with the story teller by singing along with him, asking questions and making comments for clarity, and playing roles in the enactment of the story or tale. According to Ukala, this law is made possible because, in traditional African theatre, the audience has a pre-knowledge of most of the stories as well as its interlocutory skill (the skill to interject as and when appropriate) acquired through learning the relevant principles and through practice (cited in Enita, 2008, p. 52).

Law 3: The Law of Creativity, Free Enactment and Responsibility

This law has three main elements, which are creativity, free enactment and responsibility, and it deals basically with the performer's response to the story he is performing.

Creativity

This element is seen in the fact that in African folktale performances, there are no written and memorized lines. Only the bone-structure of the tale is in the collective memory; the performer fleshes it out into a full story and, in the process, adapts new experiences to the tale, which may enhance its contemporariness and relevance to a particular sociocultural milieu.

Free Enactment

The folktale performer may break off from narrating discretionally to engage in role-play and may also encourage and engage the members of the audience in a demonstrative impersonation of certain characters in the tale.

Responsibility

The performer is usually responsible for whatever may occur in the performance process. He, therefore, must be discreet and always alert to respond to every situation (Enita, 2008, p. 53).

Law 4: The Law of the Urge to Judge

This law is seen in the fact that the African audience responds to the performer's abilities against conventional standards of performance. They also judge the characters vis-à-vis societal ethics. They make comments in appropriate audible words if the performer is doing well or not by their own evaluation (Enita, 2008, p. 55). Ola Rotimi claims that the African audience is a polaroid audience. The reaction of the African audience throughout your performance will tell you immediately if you are doing a good job. It also alerts you if you behave badly. You don't have to wait, as in Europe or America, for a critic to tell you how you did by taking it upon himself to know what the majority thinks (cited in Enita, 2008, p. 55).

Law 5: The Law of Protest Against Suspense

The traditional African audience does not like to be kept in suspense. So it asks questions which could defuse suspense. In *Akpakaland* (1990), the audience asks, "How may the poor unite and seize power?" (p. 34). In *The Placenta of Death* (1997), the audience asks, "Is Ibo pregnant?" (p. 16), "What is o-ogling? Ogling at the bottoms...what is that?" (p. 27).

Law 6: The Law of the Expression of the Emotions

The African audience freely expresses emotions such as grief, fear, sympathy, and scorn. In *Akpakaland* (1990), the audience expresses fear and anxiety when Unata is called upon to show her bottom (p. 49). In *The Placenta of Death* (1977), they express scorn for Osaze, who would not work hard and sympathy for Omon, who is being oppressed by Ibo (cited in Enita, 2008, p. 56).

Law 7: The Law of Ego Projection

Members of a typical African audience believe that they have the potential for performance and are quick to make unsolicited interjections, which call attention to their abilities. Hence, they function not only as co-performers but also as critics of the performance and performers (Enita, 2008, p. 56). In *The Placenta of Death* (1977), a member of the audience makes this kind of interjection in reaction to Ibo's incantation:

Ibo: It's white chalk that I have for she that has come.
     No one kills the teeth of laughter.

M.O.A: So this is laughter that you are laughing? (p. 15).

Law 8: The Law of Closing

This law is derived from the traditional African convention for ending the performance of a folktale. This comprises the performer's valedictory statements on the morals of the tale, using a closing formula, and the response of the audience to this formula, which may be finale applause, commendation, or disapproval. *Akpakaland* (1990) ends thus: (*Chant rises to highest pitch and snaps off. Black out. Fade on Narrator; at his back the frozen formation of cast*).

> Narrator: From there, I went from there, I returned o!
> Audience: Welcome-o!
> Narrator: (*With a bow*) Ee! (cited in Enita, 2008, p. 56).

SU, a Nigerian director familiar with Ukala's Folkist theatre style, observes that the "Laws of Aesthetic Response" constitute the performance structure within the matrix of which the director, the actors and the audience work. The actors are trained by the director to anticipate and handle, extempore, relevant interjections and physical participation, not only of the MOA, who have been rehearsed but also of the public audience. This fluidity conjures the ambience of African folktale performance, which is a new experience every time a performer performs a tale before an audience and in which the artistic event results from a collaboration of the audience with the performers. Unlike in the Brechtian theatre, in which the audience is permanently alienated, in Folkism, the audience is generally integrated into the creative and performance process, yet any of its members may detach himself/herself, whenever he/she deems it necessary, to judge both the performers and the characters they represent (SU 2017, personal communication, 21 January).

Also, central to folktale performance are the illusion-breaking techniques such as role-changing and improvisation, which allow an actor to play multiple roles and to improvise as many times as necessary. This tradition is evident in Femi Osofian's *Once Upon Four Robbers* and Sam Ukala's *Akpakaland*. Writing further on the exploration of the performer–audience relationship, the performer-audience interaction in "folkism," according to Ukala (1996), may resemble that of Brecht's epic theatre, but the aesthetics of traditional African folktales, from which it stems, far predate Brecht. The epic theatre transforms the audience member into an observer who watches from the outside and studies the performance, whereas in the folkist performance tradition, the audience member is free to choose whether to watch from the outside or from within the performance, depending on how the aesthetic and ideological content of the performance affects them at any given moment (p. 286).

As a result, according to Ukala's (1996) observations, the traditional African audience has a strong sense of responsibility to support the performance. Thus, it aims to enhance the performance while it lasts through singing, finishing the performer's lines, corrections, and praise. However, the audience also removes itself from the performance when necessary for cognition, evaluation, and critique. Folkism permits the audience to feel but sacrifices the luxury of sustained empathy, in contrast to epic drama, which exhorts the audience to reason (p. 286). SU affirms that Folkism accommodates both realism and fabulism because folktales do. Hence, folkist actors are trained in three systems of acting: the psychological, appropriate for realistic acting; the mechanical, appropriate for fabulistic acting; and the psycho-mechanical, appropriate for actions which require supplementing internal resources with external techniques. Yet, in Folkism, the set is largely sparse and symbolic because it's a run-on performance, which also derives from folktale performance aesthetics and does not allow for stoppages for changing sets and costumes. The simultaneous setting is, therefore, the norm. Ideally, the arena or three-quarter arena stage is required to simulate the village square, the front of a house, a road, or even the forest, but where that is not available and the proscenium stage is used, it is adapted to efface the picture-frame and curtain rail and action sometimes occurs among the audience in the auditorium and along the aisles. Of course, there can be no orchestra pit; its space is an additional performance area while the orchestra performs visibly mainly in the audience (SU 2017, personal communication, 21 January).

The use of the arena staging techniques, which allow for ease of setting and striking of a set, as well as an integration of the audience in the performance, is seen in Osofisan's *Once Upon Four Robbers*, as it employs a lot of the folkist theatre conventions. As observed by Upton:

> At the beginning of Part Three, a stage direction indicates that 'the text below is not rigid and should encourage free improvisation'. The Traders' Customers are to improvise their roles in the two scenes they appear in - as is the audience during the Epilogue, where it is invited to decide how the play should end. Aafa, as Story-teller, 'collects the views, making sure there is a full discussion, not just a gimmick' (cited in Ukala, 1996, p.284).

The play is set in the moonlight, and the story is propelled by a narrator who changes roles and weaves himself in and out of the story at will. The 'stage' is, of course, a bare, open space. One part of it is 'a market in a small town', the other an execution ground. No stoppages are required for scene shifting: items to be brought in by the market women are to be 'generally... easy to clear from the stage'. The execution platform is constructed as part of the unfolding drama, not by stage-hands in the dark, which gives the overall impression of an African folktale performance (Ukala, 1996, pp. 284-285). Hence, the use of the arena staging technique allows for sparse and symbolic décor, simultaneous setting, and swift-scene-shifting. SU, speaking on Ukala's folkist tradition in his directorial art, observes that *Harvest of Ghosts*, which Ukala co-wrote and co-directed with Bob Frith of Horse and Bamboo Company in Lancashire, U.K., and which toured the UK, Ireland and Holland in 1999, was a festival performance, which took place outdoors throughout its tour. In addition, Ukala sees the actor as his chief interpretative tool, yet, not as a puppet or hammer or chisel, but as a human tool, creative and interpretative in his own right. So, after his reading and analysis rehearsals, he allows his actors to further analyze, conceptualize and meditate on their roles and devise and execute their own ways of interpreting them. If an actor does this to his satisfaction, that is, meets Ukala's expectation of the appropriate interpretation of that role or even surpasses it, his comments on the actor during rehearsals would be mainly commendatory. If the actor performs below expectation in some aspects, he (Ukala) coaches him in those aspects by explaining the motivation and feeling of the character and the rationale for his action in that context; generally, this arouses in the actor the right interpretation of that aspect. If the coaching fails to hit the right cord in the actor, however, Ukala would demonstrate to the actor to copy (SU 2017, personal communication, 21 January 21). The choice of using either coaching or copying to train his actors provides them with enough freedom to take advantage of the method that will best enable them to get into character, provided they are able to play it convincingly.

Speaking on how Ukala rehearses for his folkist performances, SU informs that he begins rehearsals as a democrat to every actor and, depending on the creative and interpretative skills he finds in a particular actor, he could become a coach to him or, later, even a dictator. He usually double-cast, triple-cast or even quadruple-cast major roles to eliminate anyone who proves incapable of benefitting from coaching or demonstration. There have, however, been very few cases of such elimination due to the usual thoroughness and integrity of his auditions and casting. Therefore, he often ends up having the best actor in a role play on the opening night while the other actors play in turns on subsequent nights (SU 2017, personal communication, 21 January).

Folkscripts or folkist plays reflect the nature of African folktale composition and performance as well as some contents and characteristics of African ritual and festival performances in that they are temporal, mimetic, interpretative and synthetic, integrating speech, music, dance, mime, ritual and festival elements. In folktale performances, song and music are used not only to create mood but also serve as a means of communication between characters. Ukala (1996) asserts that songs and music frequently take the role of dialogue or serve as a soliloquy by revealing to the audience the singer's innermost feelings and characteristics. They may also strengthen a character to face a terrifying hurdle, cast a spell, or put someone in a trance. Dance and mime are forms of self-expression and mimetic action in addition to being utilized to generate spectacle. Celebration, possession, and clairvoyance all occur through dance. Ritual is used to wage mental or metaphysical battles as well as to interact with supernatural powers (Ukala, 1996, p. 285). The main features of the folkist theatre as it translates in performance, according to Ukala (1996) include:

- The folk play, unlike the other traditional performance, is a narrative realized in the performance.

- The folktale and the play are temporal (allowing for creativity),

mimetic, interpretative and synthetic.

- Unlike other African performances, the folktale is like a play because it entails much speech (p. 285).

Ukala posits that all the above features of the African folktale and its performance should be found in the ideal folkscript and its performance.

Dapo Adelugba and His "Dauduism or Adelugbaresque" Technique

Dapo Adelugba (1939-2014) was a Professor of Theatre Arts and a father figure in the Nigerian arts community. He was an actor, stage director, dramaturge, theorist, critic, historian, teacher, researcher and an administrator. Nwagbo Nneyelike (2010) describes Adelugba as "a practical man of the theatre who adapted plays for production and directed other people's scripts". A former student of his, observed that he saw Adelugba "nowhere else but in the heart of an ongoing student rehearsal" (cited in Nneyelike, 2010, p.147). This highlights how serious Dapo Adelugba took rehearsals as a dedicated theatre director.

More so, in communication with a Nigerian newspaper, Adelugba claimed that he sees himself more as a theatre critic, director, and actor. To him, theatre is play and criticism, so his area of focus is theatre arts praxis. Essentially, he believes in the indissoluble unity of theatre arts theory and practice (cited in Nneyelike, 2010, p.150). He paid particular attention to the social relevance of the plays he chose to direct. The first thing to keep in mind, according to Adelugba, in response to Ademola's query on how a director would select a convocation play for a university in the interview book

Theatre Practice in Nigeria, is the atmosphere, surroundings, and social realities of the moment. A drama that does not address the social mores of the moment is pointless (Nneyelike, 2010, p. 157). One of the good qualities of a director is his ability to maintain a cordial relationship with the members of his creative team. This was one quality Adelugba had. One of his students, speaking on his good disposition towards his actors, recounts that they were so taken up by him that they all specialized in mimicking him: his phrases, his humour and his mannerisms. When Adelugba is in a good mood, he will stutter out his joy while bursting into riotous laughing in a deep guttural voice, "Ahnhan Han, Omoburukuhanhan an huhuhu, omoburuukuuuu... where is Emmanuel Oga, please? And Marcellinus Okhakhu, Henry Foluso, Femi Shaka, Onookome Okome and Sola Fasudo... to come and act it all out" ... As the audience laughs, the old teacher will put his left hand behind his back and scratch his lower back or navel while gripping his heart in his right palm (cited in Nneyelike, 2010, p. 159).

Adelugba never showed a preference for actors who played major parts, he treated everybody equally. One of his students, commenting on Adelugba's directing style, observes that people always assume that somebody who has a big role to play in a play is the one who carries the play. But Professor Adelugba is the one who made him realize that the person who plays a cameo part (that is, the small part) is like someone who holds the key that can open or close the applause of a play. Essentially, Adelugba is obsessed with details, and it doesn't matter if you play a major role in a production. He pays attention to you, even if your duty is just to come in and out (Musa, 2006, p. 176).

Adeoye (2011) refers to Dapo Adelugba's directing approach as the "Actor's Freedom Directing Style," which allows the actor limitless power and freedom and was developed by Constantin Stanislavski. Theatre directors who use this method tend to see directing more as picturization. In reality, Dapo Adelugba defends this school of thought by stating, "I do create pictures. They are unlikely to be aware that I am making images because I do not make a fetish of it. But I am just as interested in the visual aspect of the directorial art as in the verbal aspect" (Adeoye, 2011, p. 37). Adeoye (2013) noted in his analysis of Dapo Adelugba's "Dauduism or Adelugbaresque" directing style that this method includes deliberate effort on actor training, use of good speech, democratic composition and picturization creation, intensive rehearsals, development of the performers, and development of a repertory style of theatre (p. 1).

Henry Leopold Bell-Gam and His "Aquatic Theatre" Technique

Henry Leopold Bell-Gam is a Nigerian playwright, actor, dancer and director whose directing style has accorded him international repute and recognition. He is a trained director with an emphasis on Aquatic performance and is the founder of the TESS K theatre company. He is currently a Professor of Directing in the Department of Theatre and Film Studies, Ignatius Ajuru University of Education, Port Harcourt. Bell-Gam has handled a number of positions as a teacher, consultant, and artist. His works always reflect the riverine background, and he is experienced in the artistic directions of both stage and aquatic performances. As an artistic director, he directed the Water Regatta, which entertained the Prince of Wales and Lady Diana during their official visit to Port Harcourt, Rivers State, Nigeria in 1990. He also directed the Water Regatta, which entertained President Robert Mugabe of Zimbabwe during his visit to Nigeria in 1991.

In his directorial art, Bell-Gam incorporates rituals, songs, dances, music, mimetic conversation, Laissez-Faire and Via Media theories of Gordon Craig. Speaking on the Craigian theory, HLB, a Nigerian director, who is familiar with Bell-Gam's production approach, advances that the director's function is to enable the audience to see what the playwright has written down. According to Gordon Craig, the director is the only manager and the only employee in the theatre's business and one responsible for supervising the actions and contributions of all other collaborators. He coordinates their efforts and makes sure that the main goal of this union—performance—is accomplished. In Craig's eyes, the actor is merely a vehicle through which he may project his feelings. According to the laissez-faire theory, since the actor is in direct contact with the audience when performing, he or she should be free to use their skills and instincts. While the Via Media theory contends that combining the two is preferable, letting the actor and director work harmoniously together in a manner akin to a collaborative exercise would enable them to marry their ideas and arrive at a shared concept or production goal (HLB 2015, personal communication, 2 March). Bell-Gam, employs these theories in every play he directs, depending on how his actors are quick to respond to his instructions.

Bell-Gam also claims that he has a distinctive style that he acquired via his work as a theatre director. He refers to it as the "Aquatic Theatre". When discussing the aquatic theatre, HLB points out that, just as there are stages on land, there are also stages on the water. The stage on water is called the "Fluid stage", and after this is the "Shore-line stage", followed by the "Avenue stage," which are transitional stages. This is extremely evident in boat regattas, as the paddlers on the boat execute tricks like diving into the water – This is the fluid stage. After this, the performers leave the boat and move on to the shore line, where they also enact some performances on the shore; this is the shore line stage. Then they proceed to the town, and in the course of their movement and performances, people gather around to watch them and even move along with them into the town. The performers pass through the main entrance of the town as they head to the town square. Once they reach the town square, people gather round the performers as they perform in the town square; this is the avenue stage (HLB 2015, personal communication, 2 March).

The aquatic theatre directing technique was applied in Bell-Gam's play *Orukoro*. Speaking on Bell-Gam's relationship with artists, HLB asserts that he makes sure that the welfare of his artists is taken care of. He opines that no artist would work for Bell-Gam and frown; because he makes sure he gives you a welfare package that befits your production. Bell-Gam frowns at directors who bully their artists and discourages this. For him, it is better to make the actors relax, and that is why he combines the three theories. He believes that the actor can be creative when he or she is more relaxed. He observes that Bell-Gam's packaging of artists from the University of Port Harcourt Arts Theatre to Sheffield, England, was a wonderful experience. It was a whole lot of work, but he did not do it alone; he rallied and carried everybody along, raising funds, which he used to pay for the flight tickets of his artists, their passports, their feeding, and their accommodation. Therefore, it is necessary for a director to make sure that the artists are comfortable because if they are not comfortable, he or she cannot get the best from them. Although, some artists feign illness as a way of staying away from rehearsal. Bell-Gam discourages this and advises artists to obtain permission if they cannot come for rehearsal instead of lying, and that is why he triple casts his actors (HLB 2015, personal communication, 2 March).

Effiong Johnson and His "Impact-Contact Aesthetics" Technique

Effiong Johnson is a multi-talented Nigerian writer, theatre director, actor, critic, scholar and poet. He has been a theatre and media teacher since 1984. With the accumulated wealth of theatrical experience in Nigerian theatre practice, he holds a PhD in Performance Theory and Practice that relates Grotowski's aesthetics to the Nigerian stage. He is an experimentalist and currently a Professor of Theatre Arts at the University of Uyo, Nigeria. Effiong Johnson (2003), in his book *Visions Towards a Mission: The Art of Interpretative Directing*, a seminal book on theatre directing, calls his directorial style "Effiong Johnson's Impact-Contact Aesthetics". In keeping with this style, he submits that "for impact-contact aesthetics to be realized, no aspect of the production is compromised, from the choice of play to the final summations of the theatrical pact during the dress-and-tech night" (p. 106). He says that "it is during the rehearsals that the play performance is packaged for impact" (Johnson, 2003, p.106). He explains this technique in three phases: The first phase is — orientation to the situation: here, the production script is kept aside while the actors are spelled into similar improvised situations as that of the script; the orientation therapy engineers and wires up the actor's psyche towards achieving self-revelation.

The second phase is —application to the situation. This is simply the application of the improvised aesthetics to the real situation of the production script. It is like confronting a problem with a tested and workable formula. The third phase is— acquaintance with the situation. It is directed to the attainment of absolute mastery of the nuances and intricacies of the drama. Here all aspects of the performance are given the right treatment in readiness for it to pierce the audience. This style is akin to a troupe of soldiers preparing their arsenal in readiness for a battle. The performance becomes the battle ground between the performers and the spectators, who become thrust and engulfed in the world of the performance. To attain the desired impact, Johnson adds that "the auteur-cum-subtexualistic principles are efficiently utilized, and every artillery in the performance arsenal is sharp-edged in a sensitive and targeted bravado, such that, at the moment of contact, the impact is unmistakably achieved" (2003, p. 106-107); with the impact being a memorable and a scintillating performance and experience.

AbdulRasheed Abiodun Adeoye and His "Neo-Alienation Aesthetics" Technique

Professor AbdulRasheed Abiodun Adeoye is a Nigerian stage director, dramatist and theatre theorist. Adeoye, in an interview with Nwagbo Nneyelike (2011), discusses the role of a stage director as a critical factor in the realization of theatrical objectives. He insists that "a stage director must adopt a production style". In this regard, he submits that he has employed the Brechtian style severally, and through it, he has developed his own directing style, known as the "Neo-Alienation Aesthetics". This style has twelve aesthetic possibilities, which combine to form its main structure. They include the aesthetics of the theme, song of the audience and player's systematic fraternization, multiple role-playing, artistic deconstruction, human props and demystification, multiple narrators, de-technicalization, on-stage makeup and costuming, complete instrumentation on stage, photoramic-capton's aesthetics, modern operatic aesthetics, trado-modern aesthetics and the critical recalling curtain call aesthetics (cited in Nneyelike, 2011).

This style, in Adeoye's opinion, is a blend of Western and African theatrical aesthetics. They are inextricably linked to issues around language and African colonial history. Their key tenet is that actors must be present on stage throughout the entire performance. There is nowhere to hide in this theatre. It serves as an illustration of the Brechtian theatre, in which any actor can portray any role. Up to six parts may be played at once (Nneyelike, 2011).

According to Nneyelike (2011), Adeoye used this method in the development of his neo-alienation script, *Smart Game*. Reading the screenplay, it incorporates new modern traditional dances into a cohesive presentation and employs a storytelling style that allows one individual to play as many roles as possible. While the drummers are at the orchestra entertaining, a swarm of African festival theatre is taking place on stage. In 2007, Adeoye's doctoral thesis, *Directing Wole Soyinka's Comedy on Stage*, was based on his neo-alienation theatre.

Sunday Enessi Ododo and His *"Facekuerade* Theatre" Technique

Sunday Enessi Ododo is a poet, dramatist, stage designer and script writer. He was born in Maiduguri, Nigeria, in 1962. He studied Performing Arts and Theatre Arts at the University of Ilorin and the University of Ibadan. He holds a PhD in Performing Arts from the University of Ilorin. He is currently a Professor of Performance Aesthetics and Theatre Technology in the Department of Creative Arts, University of Maiduguri, Nigeria, and has designed and produced many stage plays. He is known especially for his "facekuerade" theory, which he developed from the maskless practices of the traditional Ebira masquerades (eku), in the Ebiran Ekuechi festival, of the people of Ebira, in Kogi State of Nigeria. Ododo's facekuerade theory is particularly of great importance as it identifies the playing aesthetics and performance elements of the Ekuechi festival, which are the playing space, music and songs, dance, play-within-play, role-playing, and aesthetic supernumeraries. These are effective tools in the interrogation and reinvention of traditional theatrical pieces, especially on the modern stage. As such, directors who want to stage or re-enact any African/ Nigerian traditional performance/festival would know the directorial approach/techniques to adopt in the treatment and realization of their theatrical piece.

Sunday Enessi Ododo (2009), in an article titled "The Playing Aesthetics of Ebiran Ekuechi Facekuerade Festival", observes that "the term 'facekuerade' describes masquerades who do not wear masks but are regarded and referred to as masquerades" (p. 28). He cites the examples of masquerades such as Oloola of Ibadan and Jenju of Abeokuta, the Okelekele masquerade of Ekinrin-Ade, in Kogi State and a number of other maskless masquerades, all in Nigeria. He observes that the star masquerade performer at the Ekuechi festival, Eku'rahu (Night Singing Masquerade), does not wear a mask, as well as Akatapa (Jester) and Eku'ahete (Feet Stamping Masquerade). While the Eku'echichi (Rubbish Heap Masquerade) and Eku' Okise (Soothsaying masquerade) perform during the day fully masked in the Echane festival and also participate in the Ekuechi festival, maskless (Ododo, 2009, p.28). The idea behind the term "facekuerade" derives from the fact that these masquerades that perform without masks (faceless) do not lose their potency as masquerades; as such, the concept of mask in masquerade performances transcends the physical object of concealment, and night (darkness), voice, disguise, pseudonyms and fear become potent masking elements that de-emphasize the use of proper mask in Ekuechi festival. This informed Ododo's choice of using the term "facekuerade", which is a derivative of the words *Face, Masquerade* and *Ekuechi*, all contributing to the formation of the new term "face-Eku-rade." The organizing word 'Eku' accounts for why the word is spelt "facekuerade" instead of "facequerade". Facekuerade, therefore, means a performing masquerade character without a mask. According to Ododo (2009), "even though his audience encounters him face to face, the spiritual essence of the masquerade character is not devalued. He is still revered and held in high esteem" (p. 29).

In the book *Facekuerade Theatre: A Performance Model from Ebira- Ekuechi*, Ododo (2015) observes that "the Ekuechi Facekuerade performance has profound artistic resources and potentials as theatre. Through this, it reaffirms that the African concept of performance is communal" (p. 269). According to Ododo (2015), Facekuerade is postulated as a new performance paradigm for theatre practitioners all over the world, capable of provoking new performance sensibilities; it is also a performance form that is hinged on procession from the street to the theatre and recession from the theatre back to the street, engendering the continuity of theatre to life (p. 269). He goes on to propose a "Facekuerade theatre" model, which was derived from examining the masquerade theatre aesthetics. The study identified the diverse elements of the masquerade performance and integrates them into an organic whole - hence the "Facekuerade theatre" model. The model presents some performance aesthetic features of the Facekuerade theatre; these are Character and Spatial Doubling (this is seen as the performers and participant-audience exchange roles and space), Intermission and Feasting, Performance Motivators and Performance Moderators, Racanteur Master Performer and Imago Space Staging.

As observed by Amakulor (1987), "the Nigerian theatre exists more like an empty space with no fixed staging facilities for the audience" (cited in Ododo, 2015, p. 237). In reinventing Facekuerade theatre, Ododo (2015) proposed a spatial experimentation called 'Imago Space Staging'. It has the following features: limitless imagination, performance rhythm (songs and music), shifting playing boundaries, changing playing formations, playing adornment (lighting, sound effects, colours and scenery) and informal proxemic mode (that allows variation or violation of the strictly formalized performance structure). In this sense, the playing (performance) text is presented as a product jointly constructed by the players and participant-audience (pp. 237-239).

Imago space staging relies mainly on the limitless imaginative use of space for performative and technical requirements of the Facekuerade production. The performance rhythm is dictated by music and songs, and space is not static, as there is the constant shifting of playing boundaries and the change of playing formations, as well as the contributions made by other performance additives such as light, sound effects, colours, and the informal proxemic mode (Ododo, 2015, pp. 236-237). Consequently, four principles guide the conception and practice of Facekuerade theatre. These are:

- Flexibility in the use of theatrical elements

- Imago Space Staging (free use of space to achieve multiple focus)

- Limitless imagination

- Brilliant use of music and songs (Ododo, 2015, p. 241).

Inih Akpan Ebong and His "Cosmo-Humo Symbiosis" Technique

Dr. Inih Akpan Ebong is a Nigerian stage director, dramatist and theatre scholar. He is a lecturer in the Department of Theatre Arts, University of Uyo, Nigeria, where he continues to teach and experiment with his directing techniques. In an interview with Effiong Johnson, Inih Ebong stipulated the performance aesthetics of his directorial style in Effiong Johnson's *Play Production Processes.* He dubbed his directing style "Inih Ebong's Cosmo-Humo Symbiosis." He remarks that he has always approached aesthetics, whether applied or theoretical, from a cosmo-humo perspective. In terms of output, he sees it as a cosmo-humo symbiosis. He contends that two worlds—existential planes—human and cosmic planes—must come together to produce theatre — a concept that has influenced his artistic approach (cited in Johnson, 2001, pp. 263-264).

He explains that when he works with his actors, he wants to ensure that the actor gets to the depths of his cosmic soul in order to bring out the artist in him. And he will go to any length to realize this. The actor's ears must be physically attuned to the cosmic rhythm until he gets all of the beats, rhythms, and tempos in their proper positions, as well as turns. While doing so, he always has a holistic understanding of every tiny little bit of the action or sequence, whether it is happening on stage or backstage (and backstage can also mean the auditorium—backstage because it is not happening on stage or in darkness). Backstage thus becomes a broader concept. All of this must have a rhythmic flow. The delivery of lines, movement across the stage, turns, and gestures must have specific rhythms so that, at the end, if a professional eye is watching the play, he will have a particular rhythm or melody that is not reducible to language. It's always there (cited in Johnson, 2001, pp. 263-264).

Efua Theodora Sutherland and Her "Anansegoro" Technique

She was a well-known Ghanaian poet, author, theatre director, and filmmaker who also held academic and government positions that supported the growth of the arts in Ghana. Efua Theodora Sutherland was born on June 27, 1924, in Cape Coast, Gold Coast, British colony, and died on January 2, 1996. She went to St. Monica's School and Training College in Gold Coast, Cambridge University for her B.A., and the School of Oriental and African Studies at the University of London. She married William Sutherland in 1954, and they had three children: Esi Reiter Sutherland, Muriel Amowi Sutherland, and Ralph Gyan Sutherland.

She returned to Gold Coast in 1951, taught at St. Monica's School from 1951 to 1954; and after Gold Coast became the independent state of Ghana in 1957, she founded the Ghana Society of Writers and launched the literary magazine *Okyeame* (Spokesman, 1959). She also established Ghana Experimental Players (1958), and Ghana Drama Studio (1961). She was appointed Research Fellow in Literature and Drama at the University of Ghana (1963), and established Kusum Players (1968), a touring theatre group.

Her major contribution as a director is the giving of theatrical expression to the folk story-telling art of the Akan people of Ghana, known as Anansesem, which she calls Anansegoro (spider plays). This is clearly depicted in her play *The Marriage of Anansewa* (1987), which is based on the African folktale tradition. According to her, the Storyteller in Anansesem tells the whole story himself, and *The Marriage of Anansewa* demonstrates how this role has been adapted in Anansegoro. Anansesem is a collection of stories composed with varying performance forms and styles told by the Storyteller. Most are a combination of narrative prose and poetry meant to be sung or rhythmically recited on a solo and choral response basis. The narrator is considered the owner of the story and has the right to know everything, be personally involved in the action and be capable of inducing others to believe that they are with him and similarly involved (Sutherland, 1987, pp. 3-4).

Mboguo is a type of musical performance in Anansesem that is performed in context by members of the audience, led by the Storyteller. They are allowed to pause the story's narration and make contributions as inspired by the performance situation and some by a high-spirited desire to show off. When the music interlude is open to the public, anyone can dance; however, interludes of mimed action and comic playlets are performed by specialist performers while the rest of the assembly shares the performance of the accompanying music (Sutherland, 1987, p. 4).

A typical story-telling session, according to Sutherland (1987, p. 4), begins with a series of rousing Mboguo songs led by a specialist group's signature tune, which may be accompanied by semi-serious and semi-playful Mboguo of libation. Following that, the Storyteller begins to serialize the story by breaking up the narration at various points with different types of Mboguo, culminating with a specialist group's signing-off Mboguo song. Mboguo songs are accompanied by handclapping, drumming, percussion and gong instruments that provide rhythmic control to the performance.

Anansesem is community art, and everyone present is a performer, either actively or potentially. Although the specialists control the main flow of the action, their performance requires audience participation. People come to the performance ground expecting to be 'hoaxed' (which, in a humorous sense, is meant to be a joke in itself), and it is normal for an appreciative listener to engage in the following exchange:

> Listener: Keep hoaxing me! (*Sisi me!*)
> Narrator: I am hoaxing you and will keep on hoaxing you! (*Mirisisi wo, mesisi wo bio!*) (Sutherland, 1987, p. 5).

The above is a form of appreciation and applause, encouraging the Storyteller to sustain his artistry. "One of the many problems I have encountered in composing Anansegoro, the most tricky has been how to invest with it some capacity for invoking this element of community participation!" (Sutherland, 1878, p. 5). To achieve this, she moves to the stage, a pool of players representing both the specialist performers and the participating audience of Anansesem. The onus lies on the director to make the members of the audience feel at one with the on-stage participating audience.

Agovi (1991) adds that her first recorded attempt took place in Adropong, outside Accra, on March 27, 1959. On ground were the Ghana Experimental Theatre Players, who decided to choose a delightful open-air courtyard of an old building on the premises of the Adropong Training College and compel it to take on the atmosphere of a Ghanaian theatre. Akyea (1968) observes that:

> ... screens of woven split bamboo formed the background and to the stage, representing the walls of a courtyard. Along the "walls" were laterite-coloured seats, three steps deep, where the CHORUS would sit. These seats were representative of traditional courtyard seats round the inner walls of a Ghanaian home (p. 82).

This sitting merged well with the crowd movement, processions, and the strong presence of song, drumming, and dance. In the performance itself, a flute player strolls on to the stage, "playing snatches of folk lyrics that would be sung later during the interludes in the performance" (Agovi, 1991, p. 72). He is soon joined by drummers who play:

> ... an opening invitational sequence on their drums, and answering to their call, the CHORUS of men and women representing people gathering for a story session, made their appearances in friendly groups of twos and threes. Some shook hands in greeting each other across the stage in Ghanaian fashion. Some even shook hands in greeting with the audience nearest the wings (Sutherland, 1961, p. 47).

Sutherland believed that because of the indigenous stage structure and a flowing atmosphere of spectacle, the chorus in Anansegoro could draw the audience into participation.

Chapter 6

Directors from South Africa, North Africa, East Africa, and their Techniques

Bheki Mkhwane and His "Workshop and Physical Theatre" Technique

Bheki Mkhwane was born in KwaMashu, KwaZulu-Natal Province, South Africa in 1964. His father was a bricklayer who worked for the city's building department. He was the last of four children, with two brothers and two sisters. His mother was in charge of the household. He once saw a community theatre group, and at the age of 13, he saw his first Gibson Kente show, *The School Girl and the Taxi Driver*, in a packed KwaMashu hall. He was overwhelmed and recalls walking home, imitating all of the show's dances and songs. Later, as a child, he would watch more of Kente's work, and he would go on to learn every move and every line while performing similar shows with his community group. He graduated from high school and began working as an administrative clerk for a company, but after work and on weekends, he continued to play with his community group, of which he became the leader. A white man with a long beard once walked in and stood there watching them play. It was Rob Amato, an English lecturer at the University of Natal at the time.

They performed their play at the university. Nicholas Ellenbogen saw his work and invited him to an audition. Ellenbogen was the director of the Natal Performing Arts Council's drama company at the time (NAPAC). He trained as an actor under Nicholas Ellenbogen for eight years, playing a variety of roles in classics and world drama. At the start of the 1990s, Ellenbogen formed a troupe of five actors, three black and two white, one of whom was Ellis Pearson. In 1991, a new theatre company, Theatre for Africa, was formed, and Nicholas Ellenbogen left NAPAC to join Mkhwane in the new company, while Ellis Pearson travelled to France for a three-year training under Jacques Lecoq, the famous French stage actor and movement coach known for his methods on physical theatre, movement, and mime. Upon his return, he and Mkhwane collaborated on theatre productions both within and outside of South Africa until 2008.

BM, a South African director, speaking with DE, a South African theatre maker and researcher, on how Bheki Mkhwane works with his actors in workshops to develop ideas, observes that, first, you must have a mental image of what you want to see. Workshops involve bodies in a room, but the person in charge of the workshop must have a vision in their head. The production of *Sitting Around the Fire* was inspired by a mental image of four people sitting around a fire on the side of the road. You see this image and then begin to build it so that the theatrical moments take shape, with the actors pushing the envelope and expanding the vision (BM 2013, personal communication with DE). Twijnstra and Durden (2014, p. 177) opine that, in many cases, the workshopping process involves bringing together disparate skills and ideas to create something new and unexpected. Between 1993 and 2008, KwaZulu-Natal-based actors Bheki Mkhwane and Ellis Pearson developed a distinct style of physical theatre, as theatre lecturer Veronica Baxter notes: "Mkhwane brought the perspective of township theatre and Zulu traditional storytelling, while Pearson contributed his training with Jacques Lecoq and local university drama education" (Baxter and Aitchison, 2010).

During their collaboration, they developed a workshopping method with some universal phases of all workshop theatre. Twijnstra and Durden (2014, pp. 177-179) break Mkhwane and Pearson's workshopping method into the following steps:

- The process begins with settling on a *theme*, such as internecine violent taxi war (as in *Skadonk*), or the racial division of the poverty gap and colonialism (as in *The Hungry*) or corrupt officialdom (as in *The Hidden*).

- Out of this theme, they would construct a strong *basic idea* with dramatic potential, meaning a story with a conflict written down in one or two sentences with stock characters. For instance, *Boy Called Rubbish* tells the story of a young boy who lives with an abusive stepmother. Rubbish decides to run away, and the play follows his exploits as he attempts to find a means of staying alive. Besides a basic idea, Bheki Mkhwane explains he always seeks 'a soul image'. In *Sitting around the Fire*, it was the image of a group of homeless people sitting around the same fire every night. In most of the work with Ellis Pearson, it was the village with the stock characters. A 'soul image' is a strong theatrical image that is dominant in the work. You can step away to find sidetracks, but you always come back to this original image.

- They would then collect stories and observations that they could use to enhance the basic idea. We'll call this research *source work*.

- *Physical material* would then be collected around the basic idea, including images, props and a possible set.

- Then they would start working in the rehearsal studio, *creating the piece*. They would explore all the possibilities of the basic idea, improvise, and create situations, scenes and characters, constantly going back to the source and the theme, adding songs and movements, and improvising around their own experiences and those of others. At this stage of the work, they would not think about whether they would eventually use this material in their show or not. They would simply allow themselves to play as children do. They often called their style *'Theatre of the Imagination'* in which anything could happen (and usually did). The work relied heavily on using stock characters like the chief, taxi driver, a priest, criminals, elders, herdsmen and girls of marriageable age, intersected with the occasional stranger whose economic power and cultural differences disturbed the status quo. We'll call this the later process of building the scenes *scene work*.

- After an intense period of developing material, and based on what they improvised, they would sit down around a table and write a plot and dialogue of around 20 minutes. The piece now has a beginning, a middle and an ending. We'll call this *table work*.

- With this 20-minute piece, they would play around and discuss: What is missing? What already feels good? What can be thrown out? These three crucial questions lead them to create new material (*scene work*) and, if necessary new characters, adding situations or scenes and throwing away what was not necessary. The questions that lead the work should include: What furthers the story? What do we want to tell with this show? Where should it end? Whose story are we telling? Then it would be best if you took out what is not necessary. Sometimes you have to throw away a beautiful scene or moment because it doesn't fit into the ongoing story and what you want to express. This is known in the process as 'killing your darlings' (the things you love most), as you need to realise that they don't fit into the piece.

- After this period, they would again sit around the table and write and construct the first written draft of the full-length show (further *table work*).

- They would then rehearse it and present it to a trusted person who was, until that point, not involved in the work and could look with fresh eyes at what they had created. Based on the feedback, they would change scenes and storylines and rewrite a second draft of the piece. That second draft would be presented to a test audience, and again changes would be made before the show was finally considered to be ready and have its opening performance (BM 2013, personal communication with TR-A South African theatre director).

Given the above description of the working process, we can identify five key stages of workshopping:

1. The starting point

2. Source work

3. Formulating a basic idea about the plot

4. Scene work

5. Table work

Phases 2, 4, and 5 are repeated several times throughout the process. As a workshop director, you must guide and facilitate the process.

Speaking on how a director digs into understanding a script, BM discusses that before looking at the relationships between characters or the plot or action, you must first identify the inner conflict of the individual characters. As a director, you must constantly investigate how these inner conflicts function and how they interact with the inner conflicts of the other characters. This sets the stage for the rest of the plot to unfold (BM 2013, personal communication with DE). The foregoing shows that conflict is the driving force of the dramatic action, and an understanding of the external and inner conflict in a dramatic work helps the director in staging the actions.

Speaking on how Mkhwane develops his unique style and voice as a director, BM believes that finding your own voice in the theatre is important for everyone involved, whether you are a director, actor, or writer. By collaborating with one group, you discover that voice. Peter Brook maintains that before moving on, you must collaborate with a director for three years. When you are prepared to leave, you will have discovered your own voice (BM 2013, personal communication with DE). The foregoing offers insights on why proper training and experience are necessary for a director to find his own unique style, and this comes with years of practice, trials and errors and successes until a signature is born. Speaking on why directors must accept the reality that all too often, their job behind closed doors goes unnoticed, while the glory goes to the actor, especially after a successful performance, whereas the magic shown onstage is a product of the job of the director who works away from the preying eyes of the public, BM observes that:

> The time when the actors need to take ownership must be identified at some point during the rehearsals. Then, as a director, you can see the actors' unexpected ideas. You can now view it differently as a result.

You must relinquish control as a director and join the audience. Some directors seek to control the actors, the audience, and the finished product. To the performers, nonetheless, you must transfer this ownership (BM 2013, personal communication with DE).

Rethinking where the audience is placed can have a significant impact on how the performance engages with the audience. A venue may be designed so that the audience sits in an arena, in a half circle around the stage, in such a way that the show moves closer to the audience. This arrangement has the potential to make the theatre more lively, immediate, and communal. Twijnstra and Durden (2014, p. 165) add that the audience forms a circle around the play in the traditional circus position. A lot of street theatre works in the same way, with the audience forming a circle around the action. This is referred to as 'theatre in the round'. When performing in a circus position, the audience will always see the audience on the other side. There is no back drop, no exits and entrances, your blocking should be different, and you must use the circle and play around it. That could add meaning to your show in a way that you enjoy. This style has been used by Bheki Mkhwane and Ellis Pearson in many of their works, and the audience sitting in a circle is included in their stories as villagers at a village meeting.

Fadhel Jaibi and His "Poetics of Confrontation" Technique

Fadhel Jaibi is a Tunisian stage and film director, as well as a playwright, who was born in Ariana, Tunisia, on December 10, 1945. Following his theatrical studies in France between 1967 and 1972, he served as director of the National Conservatory of Dramatic Art from 1974 to 1978 and founded the first Tunisian private company, the New Theatre, in 1976 with Jalila Baccar, Fadhel Jaziri, and Habib Masrouki, and the Familia Productions company in 1993. He is a member of the Tunisian Academy of Sciences, Letters, and Arts and was appointed to lead the Tunisian National Theatre on July 8, 2014. He is the author of several scripts and the director of several training courses in Tunis and abroad and has written over twenty plays, including *Corps otages*, as well as four films, including *Junun*.

In 2002, he was invited as the Festival d'Avignon's first Arab creator in the festival's 56-year history. In September, he was invited by the Berlin Festspiele to create the play *Araberlin* with German actors about the aftermath of September 11, 2001. *Tsunami*, which he created in 2013, questions the outpouring of anguish that has swept Tunisia since September. In 2014, he sponsored the 76th promotion of the National School of Theatre Arts and Techniques in Lyon. *Violence (s)*, the first part of a trilogy that examines the false hopes raised by the Tunisian revolution, was produced in 2015. In 2017, he created *Peur (s)*, the second part of the trilogy, in which he examines what happened to Tunisians' hopes after the political events of 2011.

JF, a director familiar with Fadhel Jaibi productions, in communication with VAC, a Professor of Theatre Studies, observes that Jaibi's years as a student in France helped to lay the groundwork for his confrontational poetics, both through his training and his experience of cultural politics in Paris following the events of May 1968, which reinforced his belief that culture can effect change (JF 2010, personal communication with VAC, October). This experience left him with a critical stance toward political reality, which influenced his artistic choices and became a thread running through all of his productions.

Speaking of the Nouveau Théâtre, which he co-founded in late 1975, Jaibi stated, "our thinking, our approach has always been defined in relation to power itself, and in relation to the cultural power of the Other" (Boukadida, 2011, p. 78). Foreign training enabled Jaibi and other Tunisian artists to pursue a new approach to playwriting and staging. However, Jaibi stated that "every time, I was searching for a theatricality, a fashioning of fiction that would be proper to me, which would be the expression of myself, my fantasies" (Boukadida, 2011, p. 60). To accomplish this, Jaibi would draw on a technical heritage and theoretical references but create [his] own synthesis (Boukadida, 2011, p. 78).

Jaibi's theatre is always focused on current events in Tunisian society. The focus of theatre, in his opinion, should be on the contemporary in order to create polemic and provoke discussion. The forms he employs are designed to engage both the actor and spectator (Cremona, 2018, p. 73). The director does not engage in narrative performances, in which a story is told to the audience from start to finish. He manipulates his audience by bringing them in and out of the story using his own elaboration of the Brechtian Verfremdungseffekt. Jaibi, like Brecht, is opposed to realist staging. Cremona (2018) argues that Jaibi's sets are a montage of sequences that force the audience to make mental leaps in time and space. This produces a 'distanciation' effect, in which the spectator is forced to stand outside the fiction, observe it, and adopt a dialectical position in relation to what is happening on stage (p. 73). Nonetheless, Jaibi's performances reflect the world of the spectator, "engage both actor and spectator in the construction of the world each lives, dreams, and observes" (JF 2010, personal communication with VAC, October).

Jaibi uses the unconscious as a tactical space to raise questions avoided by society and to force his audiences to confront social truths that are glossed over by the false appearances of a stable and prosperous situation by generally situating the action of his plays in a dream-like atmosphere. He summarizes his vision of theatre as he opines that: "Theatre is not an art that warms the heart, that is there to please. It must inherit all that makes up man – including his dreams, fantasies and fears" (JF 2010, personal communication with VAC, October). Jaibi's poetic tactics centre on the actor's physical presence; he challenges the actor's body, mind, speech, intelligence, and emotion. His body work incorporates techniques inspired by cinematographic montage, dance, and videos. He works face-to-face with the actor and has abandoned the "crutches and props" that directors use to support the actor (Cremona, 2018, p. 73). Jaibi sees his role as "transmitting the flow to those who hold it [the art of acting] high" (JF 2010, personal communication with VAC, October).

In his work, which is at once personal and collective, Jaibi has long entertained a privileged relationship with Jalila Baccar, whom he calls his "leading actress, companion in life and muse" (cited in Cremona, 2018, p. 73). Jaibi and Baccar collaborate in the creation of the initial scenario, and Baccar then writes the script, which provides the verbal basis for the dramatic text that is ultimately elaborated through physical improvisation. Baccar has explained this technique when discussing the production *Lem*: "We start out from a story, then we come back to the characters, we tell their individual stories, giving many details, which we may or may not keep [...] Then we start improvising so that the characters can slowly take shape, concretely, that is in space, and the characters are confronted with each other from the outset" (cited in Cremona, 2018, p. 73).

Jaibi's description of his work with actors is reminiscent of Grotowski's via *negativa*: the director subjects his actors to a process of elimination in order to obtain what he defines as "the essential". Except for those produced by the actor, all visual and auditory elements are reduced to a bare minimum. Jaibi claims he learned this lesson in "poor theatre" while working in Gafsa's dire circumstances. The only ornaments or props on stage are those brought by the actors themselves onto the empty platform. Jaibi's bare stage emphasizes the way the actors fill it with their active presence through the rhythm and energy of their physical work (Cremona, 2018, p. 73). As Murray and Keefe (2007) point out, presence directs us to the actor's body and how it is constructed (p. 8). It expresses the body's openness to the immediate reality of the stage and audience.

Cremona (2018, pp. 73-47) further adds that Jaibi uses presence tactically through lighting and actor positioning, which has evolved to create scenes that look like paintings, such as in *Khamsoun - body hostages*. Lighting divided the floor into separate or single sharply defined spaces, and the alternation of light and shadow highlighted the dilemmas faced by the population in the final years of Ben Ali's rule in relation to the growing imposition of hard Islamic public codes. The minimalist stage design for the production of *Amnesia* was created in collaboration with scenographer Kais Rostom. The use of stark colours - black and white for costumes and props and gray tones for lighting created the impression of a film that was being replayed in the dictator's mind.

The artistic confrontation with political or religious control is central to Jaibi's use of text and staging. This is what underpins his artistic force because, as he says, "art is created in the immediacy of pulsions that one receives, of forces that one has to face, that can be of a material or spiritual nature" (JF 2010, personal communication with VAC, Spring). Jaibi used poetry to confront both the regime and the people. *Amnesia's* composition included extensive experimentation with forms and stratagems aimed at visually and emotionally challenging the audience in a performance with a clear political agenda.

Joseph Murungu and His "Improvisational Directing" Technique

Joseph Murungu is a Kenyan playwright and theatre director based in Nairobi with an impressive track record in drama festivals in Kenyan schools, colleges, and universities. In 1988, he was named the best actor in the country. As a playwright and director, he has received recognition for his work on *The Replay* (Kerugoya Boys, 3rd position, 1996), *Boomerang* (Kerugoya Boys, Winning play, 1997), *Fire Fire* (Kabare Girls, Winning play, 1998), *Bottom Power* (Trikha Girls, 2001), and many others. He is an accomplished drama facilitator and adjudicator at all levels. He is also an active member of the community's Theatre for Development and has worked with NGOs such as PSI and Plan International. His play *Torrent of Rodents*, staged at the Kenya National Schools, Colleges and Universities Drama Festival in April 2016, will be used in the analysis.

Murungu is known to employ the improvisational directing style in his play interpretations. Improvisation, as defined by Frost and Yarrow (1990), involves:

> Using bodies, space, all human resources, to generate a coherent physical expression of an idea, a situation, a character (even, perhaps, a text); to do this spontaneously, in response to the immediate stimuli of one's environment, and to do it a l'improviste: as though taken by surprise, without preconceptions (p. 1).

An improvisational directing style is one in which the director uses balance and body, space, movements, points of concentration, and impulses as key elements and techniques while giving directions and creating scenarios on stage rather than strictly adhering to the script. Kahuro (2018) observes that Murungu does not strictly adhere to traditional or pre-blocked directing styles. While directing, he integrates script improvement and improvisation.

Murungu also acknowledges that he combines his actors' creativity demonstrated during auditions, rehearsals, and interactions with team and friends, as well as the adjudicator's comments. This approach enables him to address relevant societal issues at the time of his production and to change the script to meet the needs and demands of the festival and his audience. Murungu is able to tap into the richness of his actors' natural abilities and diverse worldviews by allowing them to influence the theme, vision, and flavour of his work, resulting in his work being more relevant and appealing to the audience. This method also improves harmony and team spirit between the director and his cast, especially during rehearsals (Kahuro, 2018, p. 57).

Murungu worked with high school students with no proven acting experience in his production of the play *Torrent of Rodents* and had to teach them the craft of acting from the beginning. During auditions, the actors had to impress him with their voices, talent, and skills, such as dancing and singing. While mounting the production, these skills are used as sources of creativity and improvisation. After selecting his cast, he does a read-through, explaining the spine of the play, the objectives and super - objectives of each character to the actors. After this, he teaches them acting skills, beginning with basic knowledge of stage geography and conventions, as well as acting tools such as emotions, voice and speech, gestures, and body expression (Kahuro, 2018, p. 58).

With the entire cast made up of boys, he had to work extra hard to ensure that the boys cast in female roles could play the roles credibly and convincingly. He cites their eagerness to learn and experiment as a significant motivator. He sits his actors down after weeks of rehearsals and asks them to explain their roles, characters, and character relationships, as well as the play's objectives and super-objectives, to help them get into character and understand the play better. Making and maintaining the second person in an actor - the character on stage - so that he or she is acceptable and believable to the audience while remaining yourself, is one of the most difficult things an actor must do (Kahuro, 2018, pp. 58-59). He directs the actors using Stanislavski's method of acting and techniques, including the following: objectives of each scene, line of actions, the play's super-objective, analysis of text through action, truth, belief, imagination, subtext, motivation, concentration, relaxation, communion - communication with the audience - adaptation, tempo-rhythm, and the physical apparatus and movements (Downs and Ramsey, 2012).

Murungu employs auteur principles, which hold the director to be the single most important creative force in a play. According to this theory, the script alone is insufficient to achieve the play's intended vision. This means that the aforementioned skills and tools are critical in ensuring that the director is able to make a play's vision a reality (Innes and Shetsova, 2013). Murungu also employs cinematic techniques in his productions. This involves the use of film clips and images to support live drama or aid in the conveyance of previously unknown information in a play to the audience. The images and sound could also be used in a play to develop a scene-relevant agenda without resorting to flashbacks or flash forwards (Innes and Shetsova, 2013).

In the play *Torrent of Rodents,* when Mheshimiwa Bungei realizes that his wife misinterpreted what he meant when he told her to make sure she gets Mukurinowa Drama's Baby, he requests the CCTV footage to see what his wife and Mukurinowa Drama were up to. The CCTV footage is played in fast-forward mode on stage and shows all of the events that occurred a few minutes before he entered the house. Murungu's use of cinematic techniques confirms his improvisational directing technique, which involves a fusion of traditional and multimedia elements, such as electronic sounds and videos, to enhance the meaning of his play.

Run-throughs, technical rehearsals, and dress rehearsals are all used by Murungu to ensure that everyone understands their roles. The run-through and technical rehearsals aid in identifying any flaws in the production, as well as the actors' understanding of the production and the music technicians' understanding of where and when to play the music and sound effects. Dress rehearsals are used by Murungu to expose his actors and technicians. The majority of the dress rehearsals are packed with audience members so that the students can overcome stage fright and show the producer - who is also the principal of the school - how his students are doing and performing before they compete (Kahuro, 2018, pp. 110- 111).

Joseph Murungu's improvisational and experimental directing style uses the script as a raw material and guide but is not restricted by it to add necessary embellishments until the hidden beauties of the play are exposed. This approach also helps him to identify topical societal issues, which he incorporates into the script while meeting the requirements and demands of the festival and his audience.

Chapter 7

The Development of the Theatre Stage

Historical Development of the Theatre Stage

Directing involves the creative interpretation of a play-script by an artistic director, using all the available resources of the theatre to tell a story in the presence of a live audience, at a particular place and at a particular point in time. In performing this function, the director makes use of some important tools, which are the script, story or scenario, actors and the stage. The stage is the place where the dramatic action is performed. According to Johnson (2001), "wherever is found suitable for locating the action becomes the stage" (p.54). As such, the theatre houses the stage, which is the very centre of the dramatic action. Also, in the course of the development of theatre and the art of directing, a number of different stage orientations have evolved; these are the Thrust stage, the Proscenium stage, the Arena stage, the Traverse stage, and the Traditional African theatre Stage, and have demanded different approaches in terms of directing and staging techniques. This analysis shall examine the development of the theatre stage from the classical period to modern times.

The Stage in Classical Greece (Fifth – Fourth Century BC) and Roman Era (Fifth Century BC)

Plays in ancient Greece and Rome were staged in amphitheatres, which were defined by a round stage with about three-quarters surrounded by the audience. Since amphitheatres were very large and could hold great masses of people (up to 25,000), the actors could hardly be seen from far back, and because of this, acting included speaking in a loud declamatory voice, wearing masks and symbolical costumes and acting with large gestures ("Types of Stage," n.d.). The chorus was a vital part of the ancient classical drama. It played the function of commenting on the play and giving warning and advice to characters. The stage scenery was neutral and was accompanied by the real landscape surrounding the amphitheatre. Plays were performed in broad daylight, which made it impossible to create night scenes. More so, ancient Greek drama was originally performed on special occasions like religious ceremonies, and so it served ritual, symbolic and didactic functions, and the audience consisted of only freemen; slaves and women were excluded ("Types of Stage," n.d.).

Figure 7.1: The Greek Theatre

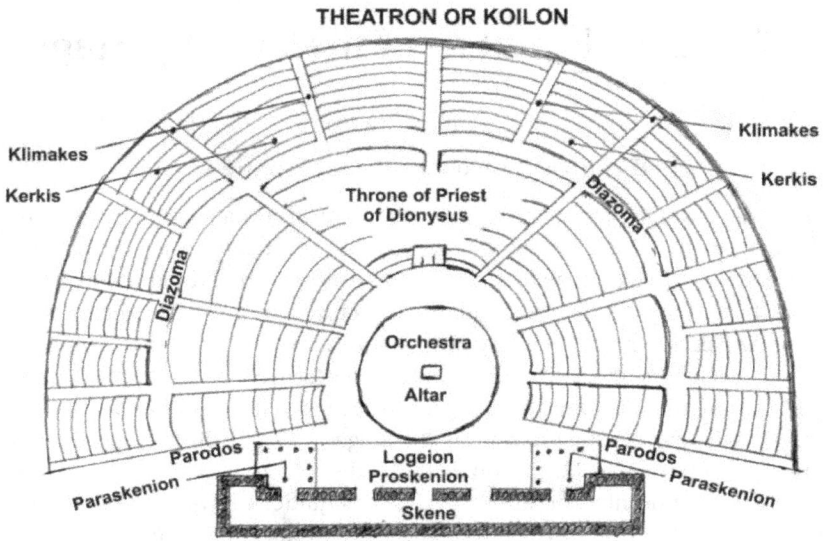

Source: Mark, 2023

Figure 7.2: Roman Theatre

Source: Mark, 2023

The Stage in the Middle Ages (Fifth – Fifteenth Centuries)

Medieval plays were primarily performed during religious festivities (mystery plays, morality plays, and miracle plays). They were staged on wagons (pageants), which were moved round the city and were stopped at strategic locations, sometimes in the market place and were entirely surrounded by the spectators. The proximity between the spectators and the actors accounted for a way of acting that combined serious renditions of the topic in question with stand-up comedy and funny or bawdy scenes, depending on the taste of the audience. Actors took into account the everyday experiences of their viewers, and there was more interaction between the spectators and the actors, as such, the lack of clear boundaries impeded the creation of a realistic illusion on stage ("Types of Stage," n.d.).

Figure 7.3: The Medieval Stage

Source: Mark, 2023

The Stage in Renaissance England - The Apron Stage (Late Fifteenth - Early Sixteenth Centuries)

The Elizabethan stage was typically found in public theatres; since plays were no longer performed outside. However, it was still an open-air theatre, as the lack of artificial lighting made daylight necessary for performances. An exception was the Blackfrair's Theatre which was indoors and lit by candle light. Theatre groups had gone professional and were mainly sponsored by wealthy citizens. As such, groups which were not under anybody's patronage or sponsorship were considered disrespectable vagabonds ("Types of Stage," n.d.).

The most common stage form in Renaissance England was the apron stage, which was surrounded by the audience on three sides, and there was still close vicinity between spectators and the actors. This meant that actors could not ignore their viewers, and theatrical devices such as asides and monologues were integral parts of the communication system ("Types of Stage," n.d.). The stage set was reasonably barren while costumes could be very elaborate, and since performances took place in broad daylight, the audience had to imagine scenes set at night, and important information was conveyed rhetorically in the speeches of characters (word scenery). There was barely any scenery, and scenes could change very quickly with people entering and exiting. The three unities were frequently not adhered to in Elizabethan drama, the Elizabethan theatre could hold up to 2,000 people, and the audiences were rather heterogeneous, consisting of people from different social backgrounds. The plays combined various subject matters and modes (tragic and comical), because they attempted to appeal to as wide an audience as possible ("Types of Stage," n.d.).

Figure 7.4: The Elizabethan Theatre

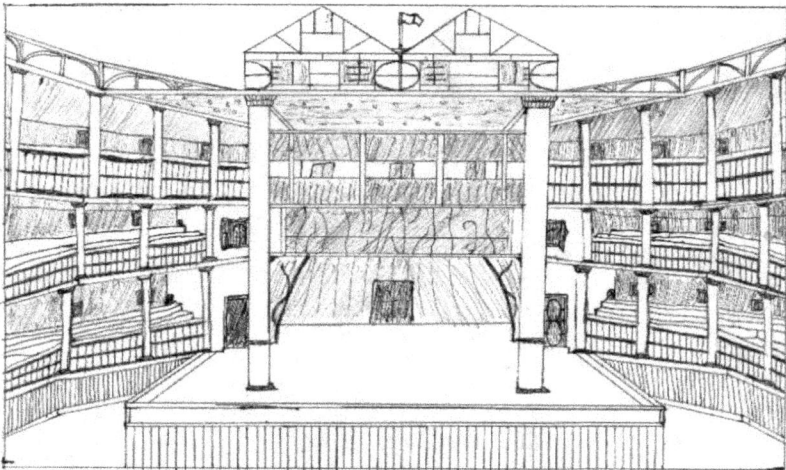

Source: Mark, 2023

The Stage in the Restoration Period -The Restoration Stage (Seventeenth – Eighteenth Centuries)

The theatres of the Seventeenth and Eighteenth centuries were smaller than the Elizabethan theatre, held about 500 people, and performances took place in closed rooms with artificial lighting. Unlike modern theatres, where the audience sits in the dark, in the Restoration period, the audience was seated in a fully illuminated room. The Aristocratic class was also interested in presenting themselves in public and attending a play offered such an opportunity. Because of the lighting system, the division between the audience and actors was not as clear-cut as we have today. Plays had the status of a cultural event, and the audience was more homogenous than in the earlier periods ("Types of Stage," n.d.).

The stage was closed in by a decorative frame, and the distance between the spectators and the actors was enlarged, as there was still room for interaction by means of a minor stage jutting out into the auditorium. There was no curtain; as such, the scene changes were done in full view of the spectators. Restoration plays did not aim at presenting the ideal; instead, they focused on highly stylized image scenery, characters, language and subject matters ("Types of Stage," n.d.).

Figure 7.5: The Restoration Stage

Source: Mark, 2023

The Stage in Modern Times -The Proscenium Stage
(Nineteenth – Twentieth Centuries)

The stage of the Nineteenth and Twentieth centuries is known as the proscenium stage or the picture frame stage because it is shaped in such a way that the audience views the play as it would view a picture. The ramp clearly separates the spectators from the performers, and the curtain emphasizes this division. Furthermore, while the stage is illuminated during the performance, the auditorium remains dark. Since the audience is not distracted from watching the play and can fully concentrate on the action on stage, it becomes clear and easy to create an illusion of real life in plays ("Types of Stage," n.d.). Thus, the scenery is often elaborate and true-to-life, with the aid of new technologies and more detailed stage props.

While many modern plays aim at creating the illusion of a story-world, as it could be in real life, and acting conventions follow this accordingly, there have been a great number of theatrical movements which counter this realism. However, the modern stage form has not been able to fully accommodate the needs of more experimental plays, e.g., the Epic theatre, nor older plays such as those of ancient Greece or the Elizabethan Age, simply because the overall stage conventions differ. For this reason, we find nowadays a wide variety of different types of stage orientations, such as the arena stage and, the thrust stage, the traverse stage alongside the proscenium stage of conventional theatres ("Types of Stage," n.d.). These stage orientations shall be discussed extensively in the succeeding chapters of this study.

Figure 7.6: The Proscenium Theatre

Source: Mark, 2023

The Development of the African/Nigerian Theatre Stage

The origin of traditional African performances can be traced to myths, rituals, worship and festivals. Performances by masked and unmasked dancers and performers in shrines, marketplaces, public squares etc., for ritual and social functions related to life, death, rebirths etc., are associated with the wellbeing of the community in the African context. According to Enendu (2002), the shrines were decorated by prominent craftsmen in the community. Best carvers and weavers from neighbouring communities were contracted to create religious pictures and carve the masks needed for the adornment and enrichment of the sacred area (p. 23). He continues that "these performers spent some days before the performance for the traditional beautician to adorn and paint their bodies, building and trying on the beads and costumes, doing the hair, and assembling all accessories" (Enendu, 2002, p.23). This formed the base of African and Nigerian theatre practice.

The emergence of Nigerian traditional theatre heralded the emergence of the Nigerian traditional theatre stage. According to Enendu (2002), the 1950s marked the beginning of Nigerian modern theatre practice as production migrated indoors to school halls, village halls, and multipurpose civic buildings (p. 23). He notes that at this time, quackery was prevalent in technical theatre practice, particularly in a few isolated regions. There was no developed technical unit, despite the fact that other aspects of theatre practice had appeared to advance, such as dancing, acting, playwriting, and to some extent directing. The stage may be left empty, student desks may be used, or the headmaster's office furnishings may be borrowed. The actors set up and modify scenarios on their own. Costumes included white garments for angels and blankets for elders. Other costumes included everyday clothes obtained from parents or relatives, and improvised items for anything out of their grasp (Enendu, 2002, p. 23). Some of the early African plays produced under this poor and lack of technical facilities, according to Enendu, were plays by James Ene Henshaw, plays by the Ghanaian Concert Party, and Nigerian Folk Opera, which were associated with names like Herbert Ogunde, Kola Ogunmola, Obatunde Ijimere, and Duro Ladipo (2002, p. 23).

According to Ogunkilede (1987), despite the obvious technical deficiencies and lack of technical facilities in some of these travelling theatre plays, much care was paid to wardrobe and makeup in order to maintain the character's statuses and personalities (p. 29). The creation of institutional theatre, which advanced the patterns of theatre practice in Nigeria, occurred almost simultaneously with the birth of folk opera and Yoruba Traveling theatre troupes. The University of Ibadan Arts Theatre, which was the first of its kind at the time, debuted in 1955 (Enendu, 2002, p. 24). According to Enendu, the first scene shop with expert stage carpenters, dressing room, costume room, sound systems, conventional theatre lighting, and control system comprise the theatre building (2002, p. 24).

According to Enendu (2002), the years 1970-1990 were the glorious years of Nigeria's theatre practice because many modern theatres were built to serve the needs of the University curriculum; among these theatres is Oduduwa Hall of the University of Ife, the two theatre auditoriums of the University of Lagos, the University of Calabar Arts Theatre, The Crab of the University of Port Harcourt, and the University of Jos Open-Air Rock Theatre. During the same time, the National Theatre in Iganmu, Lagos, as well as other states' Cultural Centres and Arts Councils, were established (p. 4). These developments paved the way for the growth of contemporary theatre practice in Nigeria.

Chapter 8

Directing on the Arena Stage

Characteristics of the Arena Stage

The arena stage is defined as an acting area situated at the centre or middle of the auditorium and completely surrounded by the audience on all sides. The arena stage is also called theatre-in-the-round, the central or island stage. The acting area may be at the floor level or may be a raised platform. One of the characteristics of the arena stage is that the stage sticks out at an angle into the audience. The audience houses the stage and sits facing it in a roundabout sitting arrangement. According to Brockett and Ball (2013), the seating is typically a stepped layout on four sides of the performing area. Seats in some arena theatres are not permanently erected, and the configuration can be changed at will, while in others, comfortable armchair seating typical of proscenium theatres is employed (p. 301).

Furthermore, Brockett and Ball (2013) observe that in the arena stage, the costumed actors, lighting, furniture, and properties usually play a more significant role in characterizing mood, time, and place than the scenery because these aspects do not obscure the audience's view. The scene designer may use a few open structures, such as trellises and pavilions through which the audience can see, but ordinarily, the scene designer depends more on furniture, properties, and treatment of the stage floor. Provision is seldom made for flying scenery, although a few architectural fragments may be suspended overhead. Occasionally, multileveled settings are used, but they must be constructed so that the audience can clearly see the action on all levels. Screen for projections are sometimes hung at various spots over the acting area, over the audience, or around the walls (the same image may be projected on different screens simultaneously so that spectators can see it), but usually, the scene designer must suggest locale, period, mood, and style with a few scenic elements (p. 302).

Also, because there is no curtain, all scene changes occur in plain view of the audience or in semi-darkness. Typically, shifting is done by hand. Many arena theatres include hallways between seating areas or tunnels that run beneath the seating and open onto the performing area; these later corridors are referred to as "vomitra" or "vom." They are used by actors to enter and exit the stage. Also, since spectators observe the play from various angles, the stage structure places specific demands on the director's staging method and the production's design to visually communicate from all sides (Brockett and Ball, 2013, p. 302).

Figure 8.1: The Arena Stage

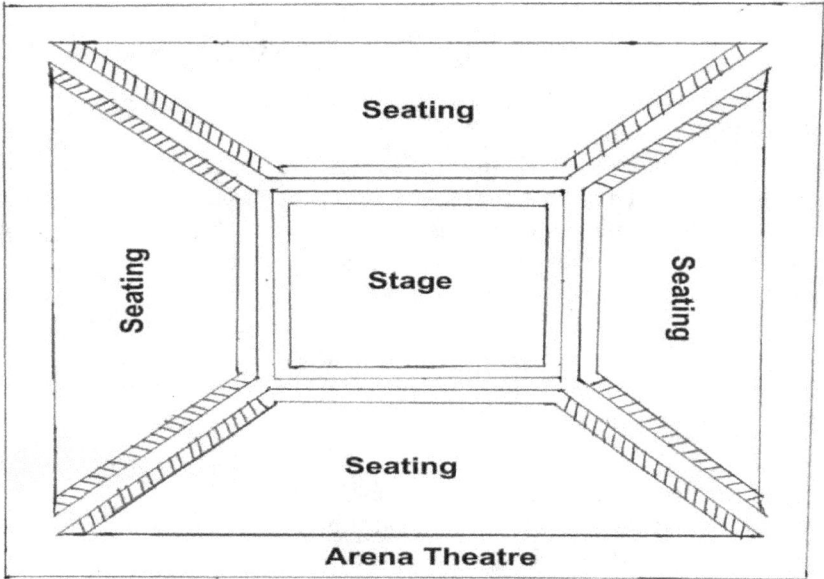

Source: Mark, 2023

Advantages of the Arena Stage

The arena stage has the advantage of increasing the level of intimacy between the players and the audience members. According to Johnson (2001), seats on the arena stage are frequently not permanently fixed; as a result, the round theatre provides flexibility in both the creative joggling of the players and the audience (p. 56). Another advantage that the arena stage has is that productions on this stage are cheaper to fund because the arena stage makes use of limited props, as heavy scenic properties can distract or block the audience's sightlines. The arena stage also creates a communal relationship among members of the audience, and this allows for an easy flow of energy between the actors and the spectators. The arena stage affords spectators a wide range of angles to view the stage action, thus giving them a more comprehensive picture of the stage action.

Disadvantages of the Arena Stage

One disadvantage of the arena stage is that it allows for too much intimacy between actors and spectators, which could reduce the level of realism or authenticity of stage productions. Furthermore, since the arena stage places limitations on set properties, productions are likely to be less realistic. Another disadvantage of the arena stage is that it creates more demand on actors and directors since movements and visual spectacle have restrictions, and the actors and directors have four different audience members to satisfy at the same time. The arena stage makes it very difficult to control sightlines or what the spectators see. Hence, it requires creativity in design and staging. Furthermore, the arena stage makes no provision for wings to mask the actors, technicians and set properties, unlike the proscenium stage, where these are available and help in facilitating the production.

Directorial Implications of the Arena Stage

When directing on the arena stage, Wainstein (2012) encourages directors to keep performers moving because if they become trapped in one position, huge blocks of the audience will only see the back of one actor's head (p. 138). Directors, he claims, can modify the sightlines by employing the following techniques: the use of levels; here, a director can sit an actor so that the audience can view the other actor over the seated actor's head. Directors can coordinate with aisles in the sense that no one sits in the aisles, thus, if an actor has his back to an aisle, there are no sightline issues to cope with, while spectators sitting along the aisle will have a limited perspective (p. 138).

According to Wainstein (2012), directors can also vary sightlines by often shifting the placements of performers or transferring them to new positions. He goes on to say that on a round stage, spectators understand that they will see the backs of players' heads, but by shifting the actors regularly, no audience member will suffer for long (p. 138). Curves can also be used by directors to modify sightlines. According to Wainstein (2012), when an actor crosses from one side of the stage to the other and then turns back to look at the actor he moved away from, his face is now visible to the audience members who were previously staring at the back of the actor's head (p. 138).

Furthermore, while directing on the arena stage, the director and the production team must know that the arena stage, aside from the advantage of creating a communal relationship between actors and spectators, puts restrictions on the amount and kind of visual spectacle that can be provided in a performance because scenery more than a few feet tall will block the views the spectators have of the stage action. More so, scene-changing equipment must be limited to that which can be put under the stage, and special effects are difficult to manage because very little can be hidden from the spectators. The arena stage also complicates the movement pattern for actors (blocking), as they must perform to all sides of the stage without having their backs to any side for too long and without preventing one part of the audience from seeing other actors as they perform.

Chapter 9

Directing on the Proscenium Stage

Characteristics of the Proscenium Stage

In ancient Greek theatre, the proscenium (Greek: proskenion) originally meant a row of colonnades (group of columns or pillars) supporting a raised acting platform (logeion), and afterward the entire acting area. A proscenium in the modern sense was first installed in a permanent theatre in 1618-1619 at the Farnese Theatre built in Parma, Italy. It had been introduced as a temporary structure at the Italian court about 50 years earlier. Although this arch did not have a stage curtain, its main purpose was to provide an atmosphere and a sense of spectacle, and scene changes were still carried out in the view of the audience. It was not until the eighteenth century that the stage curtain was commonly used as a means of hiding scene changes ("Proscenium theatre," n.d.).

Furthermore, the proscenium in theatre refers to the frame or arch separating the stage from the auditorium, through which the action of a play is viewed by the spectators. The classically defining feature of a proscenium theatre is the proscenium; an arch which frames the stage for the audience. The proscenium theatre is essentially a rectangular room, with the audience on one side facing the stage on the other; separating the two areas is an arch (the proscenium arch) through which the audience sees the action. This creates the well-known "picture frame" stage or box-set, with the arch serving as the frame for the action going on within or inside the box ("Proscenium theatre," n.d.).

Squire Bancroft and his wife, Marie Bancroft, first extended the proscenium's structure to enclose the lower side of the stage at London's Haymarket Theatre in 1880, creating a "picture frame" or an imaginary fourth wall that gave the audience the impression of spying on characters acting as if they were unnoticed. The use of controlled lighting, made possible by the invention of electricity, furthered this illusion by giving the audience members the impression that they were watching a movie rather than the dramatic action that the thrust and arena stages afforded them ("Proscenium theatre," n.d.). Thus, this made the actions onstage seem magical, fascinating, and more authentic for the spectator.

In the proscenium stage, the spectator faces the stage directly with no audience on either side of the stage; hence the spectators view the stage action from one angle. According to Johnson (2001), a proscenium stage can only be observed from one side. Since the action is focused in one direction, audience members are unlikely to squint or strain to see what's happening on stage if the auditorium is set up in tiers (p. 54). The stage of the proscenium theatre is raised like a television set which allows the spectators to see the action on stage more clearly and helps to centralize the action happening on stage. It also helps to focus the attention of the spectators on the stage action.

The stage is traditionally hidden by curtains in proscenium theatres during scene changes and intermissions before they rise up behind the arch to show the stage. The apron is the space in front of the curtain that is always visible, and some actions may take place fully on the apron. The wings are the sections behind the proscenium arch that is next to the stage but out of sight of the audience and are made up of steps that actors and crew members use to enter the stage. The proscenium arch is like a window that frames the scene; the two side walls help contain the scene, thus making it three walls. Then the wall between the stage and the audience is the invisible wall. The proscenium theatre is called the "four-wall theatre", and the term "breaking the fourth -wall" refers to actors speaking or walking into the auditorium and connecting with members of the audience during a performance.

Figure 9.1: The Proscenium Stage

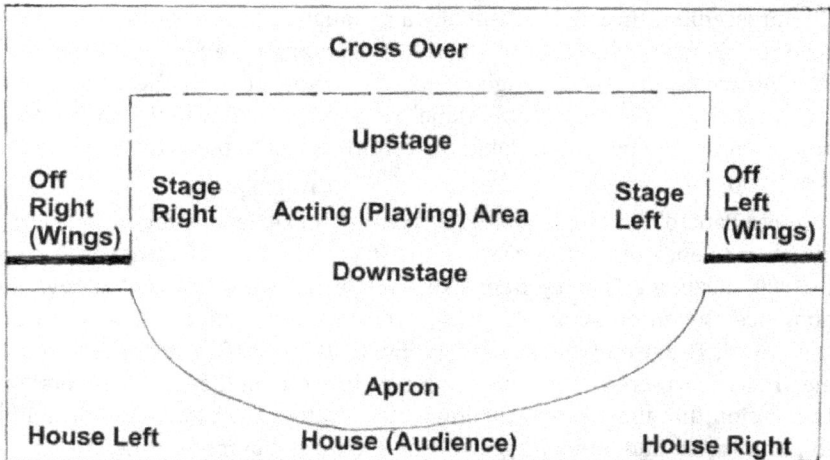

Source: Mark, 2023

Figure 9.2: The Proscenium Stage Positions

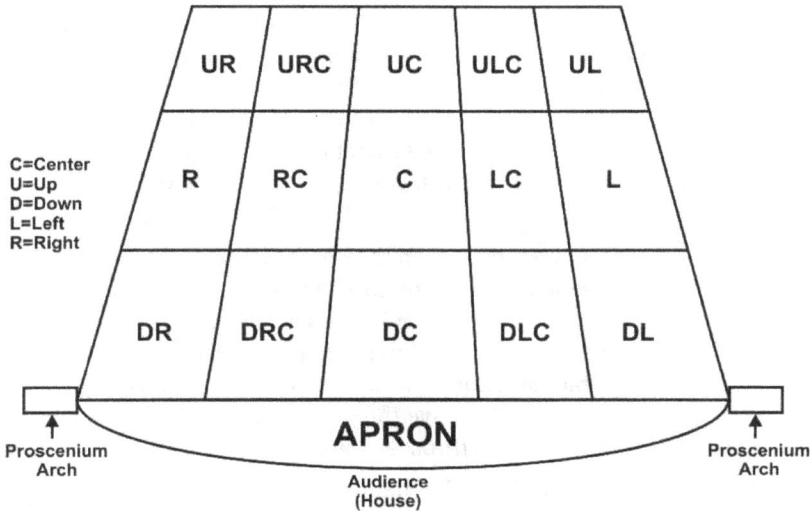

UR	URC	UC	ULC	UL

C=Center
U=Up
D=Down
L=Left
R=Right

R	RC	C	LC	L

DR	DRC	DC	DLC	DL

APRON

Proscenium Arch

Proscenium Arch

Audience (House)

Source: Mark, 2023

Advantages of the Proscenium Stage

The configuration of the proscenium theatre allows props, set properties and members of the orchestra to be concealed from the audience in the wings or near the stage, and this helps to make productions more realistic and authentic. The proscenium creates a sense of grandeur on the part of the spectators, as the proscenium arch (the picture frame) gives the spectators a sense that they are looking at a scene or a live picture. The proscenium stage makes the lighting of productions easy and beautiful when rendered properly because the stage configuration makes it possible for lights to be rigged and manipulated to create the needed mood or effect without blocking the audience's sightlines, and challenges like the spilling of lights into the auditorium are erased in the proscenium theatre.

Proscenium theatre also makes it possible for realistic productions to be achieved, as the stage allows for the use of elaborate scenery and heavy-set properties, and scene changes can be effected with ease and efficiency. The proscenium stage offers the spectators the benefit of watching or viewing the stage action from one angle, instead of multiple angles. At the same time, none is cheated or favoured at the expense of others. Furthermore, directors and actors have just one side of the audience to deal with, thereby making their job easier.

Disadvantages of the Proscenium Stage

One of the disadvantages of the proscenium stage is that stage actions can be viewed from one angle or side, thereby eliminating the three-dimensionality common with the thrust and arena theatres. Some actors and directors find the proscenium theatre configuration very limiting in the sense that actors must play at a specific location for the members of the audience to see them clearly, unlike the thrust and arena stages where actors can be seen from any part of the stage.

Because of its design, the proscenium theatre is the most expensive to build and maintain, and productions done on proscenium stages are highly capital-intensive because it allows for the use of heavy-set properties. The proscenium stage destroys the communal relationship found in the arena and thrust stages; since the stage is separated from the audience by the proscenium arch, members of the audience do not have the opportunity to view or relate with other spectators as obtainable in thrust and arena stages.

As a result of the capital-intensive nature of the proscenium stage, plays done on this stage are often written for a small number of cast and employ minimal scenery, and this affects the authenticity of productions. Furthermore, the spectators in a proscenium stage sit a fair distance from the stage; as a result, people at the back of the theatre do not get a good view of the stage action like those seated in front or closer to the stage.

Directorial Implications of the Proscenium Stage

According to Wainstein (2012), in a proscenium theatre, the audience sees the entire performance from the front. In this sense, he continues, the director is pursuing a two-dimensional, flat aesthetic (p. 137). Wainstein (2012) asserts that directors can creatively utilize the upstage area. For instance, he notes that when an actor (upstage) is behind another actor (downstage), the actor downstage must turn to face the actor upstage in order to communicate with him or her, which causes the audience to miss the actor's face that is facing upstage. If used sparingly, this can be helpful for the majority of acts, but it must be handled carefully (p. 137).

Generally speaking, directors must work to make their actors more visible to the spectator. According to Wainstein, as performers typically desire to face one another, this forces their cheeks to face the audience, which can be highly unsightly since viewers do not want to spend the entire performance staring at actors' cheeks. They prefer to see the actors' eyes (2012, p. 137). Although actors can scarcely avoid coming into contact with one another, directors must find ways to make the performers more approachable to the audience.

Speaking of sightlines, Wainstein (2012) asserts that spectators situated in front of the orchestra but on either side will have a distorted picture of the stage action because they would see everything from the extreme sides. The downstage left and right corners of the stage are where spectators seated by the sides will have their views obstructed for extended periods of time, so directors should be careful where they place players in these locations. They ought to refrain from blocking the audience's view of the performers or the on-stage activity (p. 137). Furthermore, directors should avoid actors standing in straight lines. They should use the entire stage space and create pictures that are not monotonous but varied. In terms of movements, since the actors must be seen by the spectators and they must relate with other actors, directors can employ the following movements:

Figure 9.3: Horizontal Movements

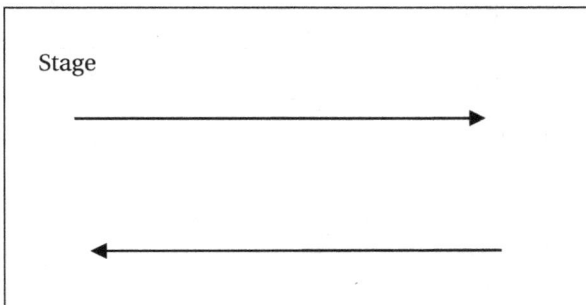

Source: Mark, 2023

Figure 9.4: Curved Movements

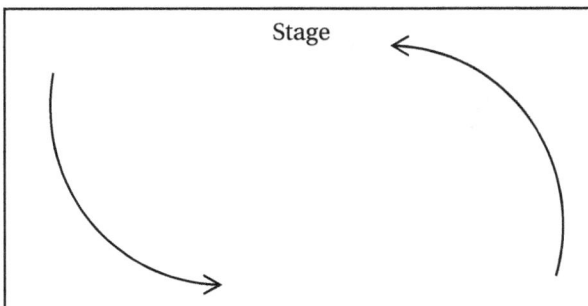

Source: Mark, 2023

Figure 9.5: Vertical Movements

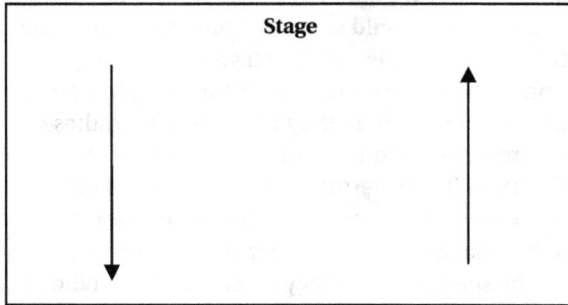

Source: Mark, 2023

Figure 9.6: Diagonal Crossing Movements

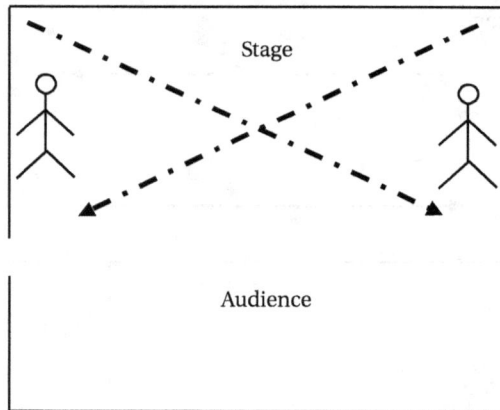

Source: Mark, 2023

Figure 9.7: Angular Movements

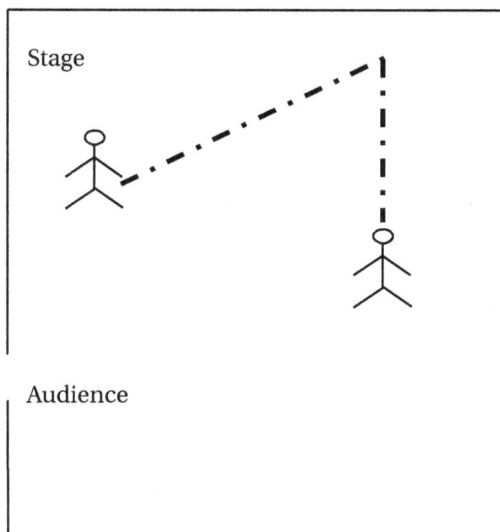

Source: Mark, 2023

For emotional scenes, it is imperative that directors explore the downstage areas of the stage. All actions must be directed towards the spectators since they have just one angle to view the stage action. Directors must strive to bring the dramatic action closer to the audience, possibly on the apron.

Importantly, irrespective of the stage configuration, directors may face challenges not articulated in this study. However, it is important for directors to always go through their blocking and should not hesitate to make adjustments where the need arises. Importantly, directors should do the following when blocking: they should know where the spectators are seated, determine the audience's sightlines, create organic action and ensure visibility, and determine the entrances and exits, as well as scene changes. More so, directors should move frequently during rehearsals to see the stage action from different angles based on the stage orientation they are working on.

Chapter 10

Directing on the Thrust Stage

Characteristics of the Thrust Stage

As described by Chatman (2014), the thrust stage is typically rectangular in design, surrounded by the audience on three sides, and the fourth wall acts as the background. It is identified by the way the stage protrudes into the audience, with the audience enclosing three-quarters of the stage. The thrust or open stage, as described by Johnson (2001), is a variation of the proscenium stage, with seats typically set around three sides of a platform that protrudes into the audience (p. 55).

The thrust stage design, invented by Tyrone Guthrie in North America, was actually the preferred format in ancient Greece and Elizabethan England because it concentrates a lot of the action right in the middle of the audience. The thrust stage is more actor-centred rather than scenery-centred in its configuration because of the proximity of the spectator to the actor, and the stage is accessed from the wings. In the thrust stage, the spectators are very more aware of themselves than they would be in a proscenium stage. The viewing angles of the spectators differ based on their seating positions. The stage itself may be elevated and is usually surrounded by a raked seating arrangement, which means that when the seats are elevated higher, the farther back they go.

Figure 10.1: The Thrust Stage

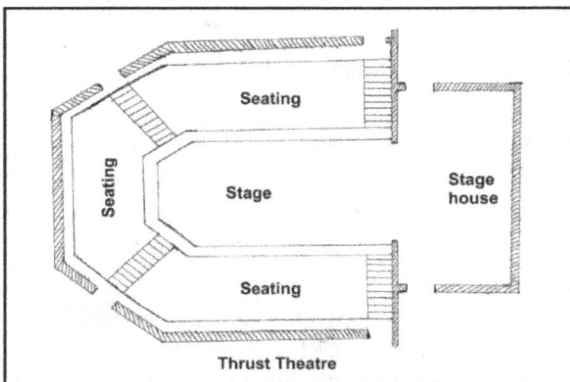

Source: Mark, 2023

Advantages of the Thrust Stage

One of the advantages of the thrust stage is that it provides for an intimate relationship between the actors and the spectators. This is because the stage is close to the audience. The thrust stage allows for forward movement into the audience, according to Martha Mendenhall (2017). The audience can feel like it is a part of the action on stage when the stage is set up this way. The audience is seated so that it can see those audience members who are sitting across the stage, in addition to the actors being close to and moving between the audience members. As a result, a sense of community is created.

Another advantage of the thrust stage is that it allows for the use of less scenery. In this regard, Mendenhall (2017) submits that, in order to establish the time and place of the action, the theatre has historically relied on the audience's imagination. But over the years, the use of scenery in establishing setting has grown significantly. Since set pieces can be placed anywhere other than the extreme upstage area, the thrust stage is not ideal for displaying a lot of scenery due to the possibility of blocking the audience's sightlines. As a result, plays presented on a thrust stage must adopt the "old school" approach that relies on audience participation and the use of few set pieces. This increases the creative value of the show while simultaneously lowering the expense of staging the play.

The thrust stage creates the feeling of a 3-D effect on stage. Mendenhall (2017) observes that when a play is performed on a thrust stage, the audience sees the action in three dimensions rather than from a flattened viewpoint. Actors occasionally arrive and exit from among the audience as they move past the audience members. Since the performance is viewed from three separate angles, each audience member is viewing a little "different" play depending on which side of the stage he or she is sitting. This 3-D interplay between actors and spectators heightens the naturalness of the presentation.

Disadvantages of the Thrust Stage

One of the disadvantages of the thrust stage is that it makes lighting complicated since you have to make people look good from the three sides, and often light spills into the auditorium. Furthermore, productions cannot have realistic energy because of the limited space available for dramatic action. Consequently, elaborate stage sets are avoided, which would have helped in the creation of a more realistic world of the play.

The fact that the spectators have a slightly different picture of the stage action is another disadvantage of the thrust stage because the spectators watch the production from three different perspectives. The thrust stage also places a limitation on how much special effects can be achieved on stage since the configuration of the thrust stage brings the spectators close to the stage. As a consequence of this, most special effects would not achieve the desired impact because of this proximity.

In an attempt not to block the sightlines of the spectators, productions on the thrust stage rely a lot on the imagination of the audience, with minimal use of set. This, thus, reduces the aesthetic quality of productions. More so, on the thrust stage, actors sometimes back large sections of the spectators, and often times directors are faced with the question of whether to block the stage action deep in the space or at its leading edge since the actors have three different audiences, all waiting to be satisfied.

Directorial Implications of the Thrust Stage

Guatam Raja (2017) in discussion with Arundhati Raja, the founder and Artistic Director of Jagriti theatre in India, provides insights on directing for the thrust stage. Arundhati Raja observes that when asked why many directors move the action of their play to the back of the thrust stage. "I need to make sure the audience on the sides doesn't miss the action," is the answer. Unfortunately, jamming the performers up against the rear wall not only results in a rather flat "tennis match" picture, but you also miss out on the immense strength of the thrust stage. Playing towards the audience establishes a powerful interaction that a director can use to generate incredible closeness and connection between actors and audience; conversely, if the play requires it, they can produce discomfort and intrusiveness (cited in Raja, 2017).

Arundhati Raja goes on to say that, as we all know, performers are never allowed to back the audience; this rule is unbreakable, even if, in our everyday lives, we scarcely notice whether anyone is observing us or if we are backing anyone when we engage in talks. Many directors are afraid that unless the audience is placed face to face with a brightly lit, clearly visible actor, they will not be engaged. The truth is that it is irrelevant. Actors can be under a shadow, turn aside, or look away from certain areas of the audience if done thoughtfully and carefully. The actors on a thrust stage may be seen from wherever in the auditorium, which is important to remember. They are not hidden by a proscenium arch or wings. Because heavy furniture and props overpower the performers and space, the thrust stage works best with lighter sets. Platforms or simple backgrounds, light furniture, or maybe nothing at all are all options. The empty stage requires strong lighting; otherwise, the space can appear flat and undescriptive (Raja, 2017).

According to Arundhati Raja, "it is important that actors only make meaningful movements and significant gestures or don't move at all. A good actor can deliver a long speech, if needed, with their back to the audience. But if it is used merely as a device with no real relevance to the contextual situation at that time, it will be irritating to the spectators. What works best is text-driven movement" (cited in Raja, 2017). When blocking on the thrust stage, Arundhati Raja advises directors to use the radius/diagonals of the stage. They should have actors move in curves of the stage or around furniture rather than in straight lines. Actors should be aware that there are people stage right and stage left and not play out to the central portion only. The downstage centre area of the stage is ideal for scenes that call for emotion, introspect and conflict. It allows the actors to truly use significant gestures and move meaningfully. If they are so close to the audience, it is even more essential. The upstage area is great for more static situations; when required, it can be very powerful to have an actor static upstage watching a more dynamic scene happening downstage (cited in Raja, 2017). Importantly, when interpreting a text, it is important for directors to think of the space, as most plays can be adapted to the available space, and it is pertinent to always look at characters and their motivations when blocking.

Wainstein (2012) observes that the thrust stage has an upstage region that is viewed from the front by the audience, similar to the proscenium (p.139). He also claims that while staging on the thrust's upstage region, the rules for proscenium apply. On the thrust, the rules of 'in the round' apply with the caveat that there are only three sides to be concerned with instead of four; he adds that while using the downstage areas, directors should avoid playing everything upstage; they should use the thrust area fully, bringing the show close to the spectators and fully utilizing the entire stage area (Wainstein, 2012, p. 139).

According to Wainstein (2012), the scenery might be transported downstage from the rear or through the aisles. He advises directors to keep the scenery on the thrust simple, similar to the arena stage, and to avoid staging all situations to favour the front or centre audience. He considers all three sides to be the "front," and directors must balance their usage of each (p. 139). In terms of entrances and exits, Wainstein (2012, p. 139) claims that entrances can be made from the upstage area, through the aisles to the sides, and through the front corners of the rectangular thrust. He argues that directors should use the thrust dynamics to enhance the relationship between actors and spectators. The thrust stage 'thrusts' the play closer to the audience, and there is power in that.

Chapter 11

Directing on the Traverse Stage

Characteristics of the Traverse Stage

The traverse stage is a stage in which the audience is seated on two sides of the stage, facing each other, with the stage in between them. It is also known as the corridor or alley stage. This is the type of stage used for runway or catwalk shows. According to Vertesi (2017), the audience is placed on two opposing long sides of a rectangular stage on the transverse stage. Though a lot of theatres have minor variants on this arrangement with additional levels and stage sections, a real traverse stage has only one central platform. Some traverse stages resemble a thrust or three-quarter round stage because one end of the stage space may also end in the audience. Sometimes the stage's ends are considerably larger than the traverse itself, providing additional room for the actors, the set, and the scenery. However, directors do not frequently use this stage for play production.

Figure 11.1: The Traverse Stage

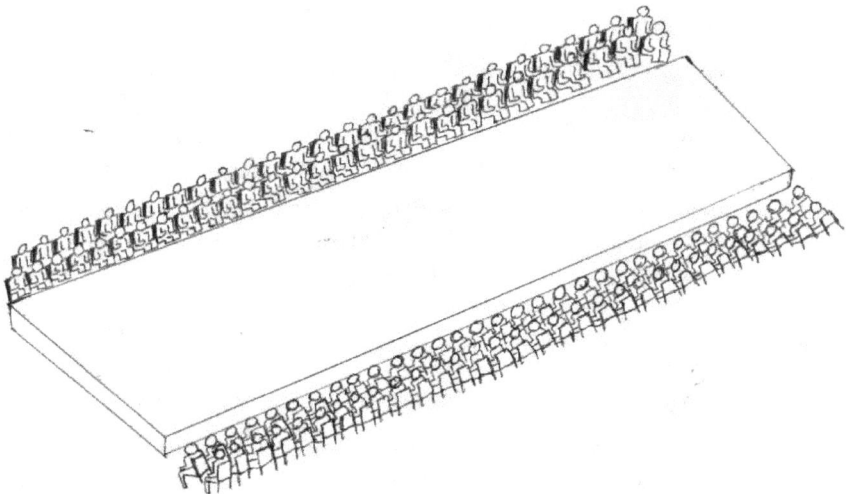

Source: Mark, 2023

Advantages of the Traverse Stage

The traverse stage makes members of the audience feel more involved in the stage action, especially in scenes of confrontation, especially fight scenes. It is ideal for low-budget productions because it allows for minimal use of scenery. Because of its runway characteristics, its catwalk feeling allows for dynamic, fast-paced entrances and exits, depending on what the director wants. The traverse stage provides for a more intimate relationship between the performers and the spectators, and another advantage it has is that it is relatively unpopular when it comes to play productions when compared with other stage orientations; as such, it provides directors with a virgin ground to test new staging techniques.

Furthermore, the traverse stage allows for greater projection of voice on the part of actors, thereby giving the audience the benefit of hearing them more clearly. The traverse stage, because of its nature, leaves every action visible to both the performers and the audience. It allows for intimate staging. As such, the audience gets more involved in the stage action.

Disadvantages of the Traverse Stage

The traverse stage allows for intimacy between the actors and spectators, and too much intimacy can reduce the authenticity of productions, especially when there is the need to create special effects. The traverse stage favours minimalist productions, and the idea of minimalism in terms of the use of props can make productions seem half – real (simplified realism – a situation where directors use half of what is real).

This stage orientation is unpopular because of its nature, and most directors find it unsuitable for theatre productions, which makes it less preferable. Another challenge of the traverse stage is that once an actor walks past one part of the audience, the actor's back will be to the audience.

It also makes the placing of scenery on stage challenging. As such, most set properties are placed at the far ends of the stage to avoid blocking the sightlines of the spectators. Also, most traverse stages are usually elevated, and most times, people in the front row may not be able to see the stage action very clearly except they stretch.

Directorial Implications of the Traverse Stage

Vertesi (2017) comments that it is obviously difficult to construct a traditional set or backdrop on a transverse stage. Because this stage orientation is treated in the same way as a theatre-in-the-round, the scenery must be basic, transparent, and three-dimensional. In the realm of sound, Vertesi (2017) adds that directors and sound designers must be aware that the sound reinforcement concerns of the traverse stage are troublesome because speakers facing one side of the audience also face the stage and are prone to feedback. As a result, finding angles for acceptable stereo mixing is nearly impossible, and there can plainly be no separation between a stage monitor mix and an audience mix. As a result, because many traverse theatres are small, many sound engineers prefer not to mike traverse plays at all.

Because performers can be observed from two sides, Vertesi (2017) recommends lighting with depth. This indicates that lighting the performers from at least three dimensions (from above and from two sides), preferably the audience's sides, and utilizing a light-coloured stage surface, allows light to bounce off the floor.

Directors must also appreciate that the traverse stage, like the theatre-in-the-round stage, provides some staging issues. According to Vertesi (2017), the first problem is the lack of downstage areas because audience members are on either side of the stage and have potentially conflicting viewpoints of an actor, raising the dilemma of which direction the actor should face when delivering his or her speech to the audience. In tackling this challenge, directors must apply wisdom and never allow actors to back one side of the audience for too long, hence, their rendition of lines and execution of movements must be varied and evenly distributed to both sides of the audience.

Chapter 12

Directing on the African Traditional Theatre Stage

Characteristics of the African Traditional Theatre Stage

African traditional theatre refers to those forms of entertainment and theatrical nuances that were in existence before the colonization of Africa by the Europeans. African traditional theatre, according to Krama (2006), is an expression of the people, institutions, and experiences of the African society (p. 3). African traditional theatre incorporates traditional or cultural festivals. Commenting on the Nigerian scenario, Ebo (2012) states that live theatre is as old as Nigerian society because the pre-colonial theatre, which was anchored in the people's antiquity, was a live theatre. African traditional theatre manifested itself in festivals, initiation rites, dance, mime, and other rituals that marked the birth and death of every African (p. 170).

African traditional theatre originated from the ritualistic practices of Africans, just like the Greek theatre. The places of performances included shrines, burial grounds, forests etc., where rites and other traditional ceremonies were performed. Bakery (1982) remarked that African traditional theatre is not limited to rites and festivals but also to secular activities such as storytelling and a variety of genres. It might be a truly tragic scene presented by a performer to whom the audience listens and applauds, and encourages with laughter (quoted in Krama, 2006, pp. 8-9).

Krama (2006) opines that African traditional theatre contains not only ritual material but also storytelling and the retelling of myth and history. There are two types of African traditional theatre: secular and religious. In the context of their origin, holy forms are theatrical forms linked to religious events. These include things like rites of passage and propitiation. Outsiders are sometimes barred from attending these shows. In contrast, secular forms refer to rituals, religious rites, and activities that fulfil dual meanings. They can still be associated with worship but can also be conducted outside of it. The majority of secular forms are myths and stories derived from religious rites or life processes (Krama, 2006, pp. 9-10).

African traditional theatre thrives in the communal nature of the African society. It does not seek to alienate the individual as is common with the Western theatre but strives to reintegrate the individual back into the community. As such, African theatre thrives in communal existence. The structure of the African theatre is cyclical and not lineal, as is evident in Western theatrical structures. The Western theatre, in terms of structure, terminates at the denouement, which may alienate the individual and the community. However, African theatre extends into reincorporation expressed in feasting and convivial gamos, which celebrates the oneness of the community despite the extent of demise or defeat. African theatre has a three-dimensional structure of opening (separation), performance or action (threshold) and gamos or resolution (reincorporation), which extends beyond the confines of structured time, location and theory (Krama, 2006, p. 14)

Krama submits that African traditional theatre has evolved into a modern theatre which has two categories: Popular or Folk theatre and Literary theatre. The popular or folk theatre as a genre of African theatre developed from secular rites and thrives more in urban centres. It draws heavily from oral tradition and festivals. The folk or popular theatre was popularized by Hubert Ogunde, Duro Ladipo etc. The Alarinjo, Kwahir, Khana/Bornu Puppet and Wizzy are examples of folk theatre. In contrast, the Literary theatre is a genre of African theatre styled after European theatre models in terms of content and structure. The themes range from adaptations of European stories in African settings or exploitation of African folk stories based on European structures (2006, p. 11).

The elements of African theatre include Rituals (libations, festivals, magic, spell, masquerade), Speech Surrogates (chants, prayers, songs, riddles and incantations), Instrumental sounds (signals, flutes, drums, bells, rattles etc.), Costumes (masks, stools, skins, weapons, clothes, live animals, tattoos, scarification etc.), Drums, Audience, Actors, gods etc. Legends and myths are strong elements of African traditional theatre and drama. Legends are stories about historic personages handed down by tradition, which is believed by many but cannot be proven to be true, while myths are tales about a hero or the early history of a people, usually involving supernatural beings and events. When certain activities or events become outdated, they serve as references or myths (Krama, 2006, p. 23).

The audience of African traditional theatre is part of the performance (participant-audience). The audience consists of members of the community, and they make contributions to the creation of the performance. The performance mode of African traditional theatre can be christened "festival theatre". Ola Rotimi used this term to describe his directing style, which was more like a reenactment of African communal experiences. Although in an African traditional performance stage, the acting area is clearly defined by the nature of the performance space, the flow of the performance or rites clearly defines the actors and the audience, even if there is the absence of an arch separating the spectators from the performers; one can distinguish the audience from the actors.

Human actors, audience actors, and spirit actors are all part of traditional African theatre. According to Krama (2006), human actors have no limitations in terms of number or gender, as both male and female performers play complementary roles. Depending on the role and nature of the performance, the Chief Priest or the main actor may be male or female. Female roles are prominent in the Gbogo Ko and Iria ceremonies of Ogoni, Kalabari, Abua and Odual. Although males wear masks in masquerade performances, ladies may be attendants or dancers (p. 31). He adds that the human actors include dancers, drummers, mask carriers, attendants, choric groups and the audience. At some points, the distinction between the audience and the prominent actors become fluid. The audience may join in the dance or may interrupt the performing area to cheer or paste money on the performers or give them gifts. At this point, it becomes difficult to distinguish between the spectators and the actual performers. The spirit actors — the gods, spirits and ancestors — are also believed to be actively present in the performance.

Sometimes, the gods become physically visible by the presence of a masquerade or totem, and sometimes invisible only to be communicated with through signs or mediums like the priests. The audience actors comprise the people who gather to watch the performance without participating (nominal audience), the audience who actively participates in the performance (participant-audience), and the spirit audience, which represents the presence of the gods and ancestors, which are believed to be present, supervising the performance (Krama, 2006, p. 31).

The African traditional theatre stage varies according to the type of performance. The African stage can be aquatic, as in most shows, or an isolated camp or a forest for initiates. In most performances, as Krama (2006) observes, the stage or location of the performance has great significance and honour, and most performances are done at the shrine, playground, or on the street. The shrine of the supreme deity, which draws the people together for worship, judgment, or entertainment, is typically located in the arena, which serves as the main performance space. The venue for the performance could be a family or compound shrine, and it represents the connections among the main social classes, their ancestors, and the channels of communication that exist between people (2006, p. 34).

African traditional theatre has four types of stages: The Fluid Stage, The Shoreline Stage, The Avenue Stage and The Arena Stage: The Fluid Stage: Is derived from the aquatic stage. For the aquatic environment, water is a convenient performance area. In this type of stage, the performers are submerged in water while the masks carried by them float and are very visible to the audience. The Shoreline Stage: This is another derivation of the aquatic stage. The shoreline stage is the beach. An essential aesthetic feature of the fluid stage is the movement of the masked performance from the fluid stage to the floating stage and to the shoreline from where the performers move to the shore. The Avenue Stage: The avenue or street, or parallel stage, is the route through which the performers pass to the arena. The performers display with the audience standing on both sides of the route. Usually, this stage is a mobile stage. The Arena Stage: The arena stage or theatre-in-the-round is a common stage in traditional African theatre performances. The arena is usually the ancestral meeting place which contains the shrine or the market. It transforms into a stage when the audience surrounds the performers. The shrine may be the only permanent structure of the arena stage (Krama, 2006, p. 35).

African traditional theatre thrives on the concept of "total theatre". This is because African traditional theatre represents the shared experiences of the group life, the institutions derived from the group life and the values and rapport essential to the continuity of the group. The idea of total theatre means a theatre presentation that has the assemblage of all the elements of theatre in a final performance. It pays less attention to the written text and emphasizes the use of all or most of the theatrical elements such as music, dance, song, story, mime, spectacle, costume, make-up, special effects, drumming etc. An example of the African traditional theatre stage is the Ekuechi Facekuerade Performance stage.

Figure 12.1: Ekuechi Facekuerade Performance stage

Source: Mark, 2023

Advantages of the African Traditional Theatre Stage

The African traditional theatre stage favours the spectators because it destroys the traditional arch that separates the actors from the spectators in conventional stage orientations. Hence, the spectators are active participants in African traditional performances. Unlike Western stage orientations, African traditional theatre allows for performances on land and water, as seen in aquatic theatre. The African traditional theatre stage allows for much flexibility in the nature and use of the performance space, as most African performances take the form of arena staging and may not need the use of lavish set properties. In some cases, a shrine may be the only permanent structure. And usually, actors and participants may have to move from one performance locale to another.

The traditional African theatre stage is not a structure or conventional theatre house built in which spectators must pay a stipulated amount before they are admitted. It is accessible to everyone in the community. Although in most African performances, women are not allowed to participate. However, the performance is derived and owned by everyone in the community.

In terms of staging, it can be argued that African traditional theatre performances are cheaper to fund than conventional theatre productions, as most of the paraphernalia needed for the performances are provided by the local townspeople. Materials for staging might include wood, Indian bamboo, raffia palm, mud, thatch and wattles etc.

Disadvantages of the African Traditional Theatre Stage

The African traditional theatre stage destroys the traditional demarcation between actors and spectators in conventional stage orientations; consequently, separating the actual performers from the spectators may be difficult. The African traditional theatre stage cannot survive harsh weather conditions due to the nature of the materials it is composed of. Consequently, such environmental and weather conditions as rain and harmattan may negatively impact on the performance venue or space, especially if the venue is a burial ground, a playground, or a roadside.

African traditional theatre lacks the convenience provided by conventional stage orientations, especially because of the presence of good theatre seats, lighting equipment, air conditioners etc., that help to ensure the comfort of spectators. In traditional African theatre performances, spectators are expected to stand or move about following the performers as the performance dictates, while others may retire to take shelter under surrounding buildings, trees etc.

African traditional theatre stage is not designed to accommodate conventional stage plays, although it is suitable for unscripted performances, in which case the director may have to adapt the performance to suit the locale. In African traditional theatre, one cannot boast of the existence of a professionally trained scene or set designers that cater for every need of the performance space or stage. However, some persons perform these functions and can stand in as set/scene designers at the local level.

Directorial Implications of the African Traditional Theatre Stage

In Africa, controversies have reason among scholars regarding the place of the director in African traditional performances. While some believe that the director exists in traditional African performances, others are of the opinion that he does not exist, premised on the belief that African traditional performances do not qualify as theatre. Interestingly, Nigerian theatre scholars such as Wole Soyinka, Ola Rotimi, Kalu Uka, J.P. Clark, J. A. Adedeji, J.N. Amankulor, Micheal Echeruo, Oyin Ogunba, Oyekan Owomoyela, and Euro - American African theatre sympathizers such as Micheal Ertherton, Ruth Finnegan, Peter Johnathan, Berth Lidfors, James Gibbs and many others have risen up to defend the position that African theatre does exist.

Speaking on the controversy regarding the place of the director in traditional African theatre, Adeoye (2010) points out that it is intriguing to note that the presence of the theatre director in traditional theatre or otherwise, has always been a contentious issue. Theatre scholars such as Nzewi (1979), Adedeji (1981), Amankulor (1981), Akinwole (2000), Ejeke (2000), Bakare (2002), Ogundeji (2003), Bell-Gam (2003), and others support the idea that the theatre director is eminently present in the traditional African theatre, but Finnegan (1970), Echeruo (1971), Gbilakaa (2000) and others vehemently disagree (p. 85).

Supporting the existence of the director in traditional African performances, Bell-Gam (2003) argues that "the master-drummer (Akwafaribo) who uses drumming to influence, detect time, punctuate the performance of a masquerade in the Nji-Owu performance of Opobo, in Rivers State, is also a director" (p. 9). Adedeji (1981), speaking on the Ologbin Ologbojo, the founder of the Alarinjo Theatre; a traditional Yoruba travelling theatre as a director, observes that the Alarinjo Theatre was founded by Ologbin Ologbojo. As a worshipper of Obatala and the Oba clan, he established the theatre as a constant component of court entertainments because of his hybrid son, Olugbere Agan. Ologbin Ologbojo hired the master carver Olojowon to craft a wooden face mask and the costume designer Alaran Ori to create a set of clothes for him. With these, Olugbere Agen performed as both a strolling player and a costumed actor. While the Akunyungba, the royal rhapsodists, provided the choral chants, Ologbojo functioned as the masque-dramaturge or animator (pp. 223-224). The above description of the duties of the Ologbin

Ologbojo matches some of the duties of a director, as there existed playwright-directors in the classical period who did not only create the stories of their plays but took charge of the management and staging of their productions in which they also performed. This researcher, therefore, agrees with the position that the director exists in traditional African theatre.

In addition, in most African traditional performances, some scholars say it is the Chief Priest, choreographer, drummer or senior member of the group that performs the role of the director. Bell-Gam (2003) claims that an Akwafaribo in Rivers State, Nigeria, is a director in his own performance rights, using the Nji-Owu masquerade performance of Opobo. He comments, "the organization of cultural groups is not a new phenomenon in the cultural history of Nigerian rural communities" (p.9). Long before European colonialism, Nigerian rural communities had various kinds of cultural groups, with leaders who coordinated them. In Benue State, such a person is called the "Kwagir" by the Tiv people. Among the Ibos, he is referred to as the "Isi egwu". The Ibibios call him "Akwa uneg", the Isokos call him "Osu", the Kalabaris call him the "Kuku faribo Iyala". While in Opobo town, the person who handles such responsibilities is the "Akwafaribo", the master drummer.

According to Bell-Gam (2003, p. 10), the Akwafaribo's primary responsibility is to coordinate, supervise, discipline, inspire, motivate, and order the entire cultural troupe in order to ensure a successful performance. The ability to drum has been passed down from generation to generation, and even if an Akwafaribo lacks formal art training, he is nevertheless able to creatively instruct, supervise, and organize people to the enjoyment of the audience. In her discussion of the characteristics of the African traditional artist, Helen Chukwuma (1994) notes that the traditional artist is thus every man and any man or woman who is sufficiently knowledgeable in the literary traditions of the African people and capable of conveying this to an audience in a fun way (cited in Bell-Gam, 2003, p. 10). For Bell-Gam, the words 'literary traditions' would be valid if they were substituted with oral traditions.

Bell-Gam (2003. p.11) observes that the Akwafaribo (master drummer) takes on numerous tasks in order to achieve the beauty of the performance and its acceptability to the audience. He is aided in his directorial activity by Oru-Ogolo (singer) and Owu-Korigbo (masquerade leader). In Nji-Owu performance, the Akwafaribo (master drummer) chooses the performers through an audition procedure that includes young males for the masquerades, maidens for the dancers (Owu-Korigbo), and vocalists; the best of the singers is chosen as the Oru-Ogolo. Oru-Ogolo, a female, rehearses with the maiden dancers because women are not permitted in the "Ikina" masquerade home, where rehearsals are generally held at night. The night before the public performance, the Ikina (Masquerade cult members) conduct a night vigil after an exhaustive rehearsal, performing all rites and sacrifices required to placate the water spirits. The masquerade headgear, costumes, and properties are all prepared that night, all under the supervision of the Akwafaribo.

The cultural group begins its quiet tour of the town at 5 a.m., while people are asleep, with extremely spiritual melodies that are performed intermittently, interwoven with drumming. "Ijumangi" is the name given to this procession. It performs three functions. For starters, it is a rite that announces the presence of water spirits in the village. Secondly, it is an excellent advertisement tactic in an oral context. Thirdly, members who were absent from rehearsals without permission are visited and sanctioned that morning. By 6 a.m., the masquerades and other performers, including maiden dancers and singers, are dressed in their full colourful costumes and regalia. Following a brief pause at the shrines, the Ijumangi group joins them for a formal entry into the arena. A whole performance is held in the arena, which has also been built to create the ambience of a typical aquatic habitat. Few people, mostly children, attend this early morning show. The real performance takes place between 4 and 7 p.m (Bell-Gam, 2003. p.11).

According to Bell-Gam (2003), another aesthetic quality of Nji-Owu performance which justifies the Akwafaribo as a director is the blocking of the arena. Deep sea, shallow areas, shrine grooves and mangrove shores are demarcated with the use of sea plants and trees. Each fish masquerade is placed at the appropriate habitat through mime swimming movements into the main open arena (waterfront) in search of other smaller fishes to feed on. The drummers, maiden dancers and the singers occupy the same stage area. The Owu-Korigbo shares the same space with the masquerade because of their protective function to the masquerade (pp. 11-12). Bell-Gam (2003) further observes that a major aesthetic difference between directing in conventional theatre and that of Nji-Owu performance lies in the directional time span of the two. While in the conventional theatre, the process of directing ends at the technical rehearsals, directing in the Nji-Owu performance progresses into the main public performance; although one may argue that prompting an actor during a public performance is part of directing, it is essential to note that the prompter is not the director. The key elements that dominate the staging of Nji-Owu performance are music, dance, mime and song. With music, the Akwafaribo dictates the dance steps, punctuates the mime actions and harmonizes the rhythm of the songs. Examples can be drawn from his directional music concept of mime in the sequence of the performance (p. 12).

As already stated, directors must note that when reinventing African traditional performances, space is determined by the type of performance enacted on it. More so, the staging style of traditional African theatre is the processional and arena staging technique. Idemudia (2012) notes that performances on African performance space are flexible and permit mobility from one area of a community to another. These are often procession-style movements that start at a shrine, proceed to the home of the traditional monarch, before ending at the market square (p.157). A typical example of the procession and staging of an African traditional performance is seen in the Ebiran Ekuechi Facekuerade festival of the people of Ebira, in Kogi State of Nigeria.

Figure 12.2: Procession and Staging of Ekuechi Facekuerade Performance

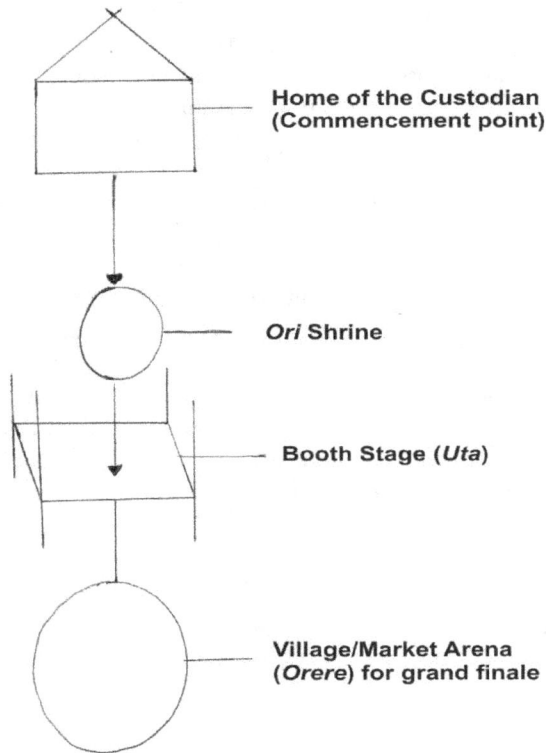

Home of the Custodian
(Commencement point)

Ori Shrine

Booth Stage (*Uta*)

Village/Market Arena
(*Orere*) for grand finale

Source: Mark, 2023

The space utilized for traditional African performances are not restricted to a specified environment or locale; hence, its space is defined and determined by the procession and everything it embodies in its pathway.

According to Dauda Enna Musa et al. (2006), the African actor exploits the natural performance space while performing in a way that is a combination of an acrobat, a musician, and a dancer. He performs in front of a beautiful natural setting that is always a comfortable playground. This necessity and the actor's performance serve as the foundation for the African notion and use of space. He indeed requires space for all of his acrobatic acts (cited in Idemudia, 2012, p. 157).

At every level of performance, there is usually a performer along with a procession of onlookers who are either fully or partially involved in the performance. As the procession moves with the performance, every space utilized by everybody involved in the experience translates into a performance space. The scenic design is accentuated by the presence of humans, the natural groves and the surrounding environment. In this case, each moment of performance is done in a transit space fluid and devoid of any form of gulf or restriction from the audience, who like the performer, moves from one performance space to another in time. Kinetic Scenery is the term Enendu Molinta (1996) uses to characterize the contemporary scenic architecture for such fluid performances. He defines it as consisting of scenic elements that visually enhance the dramatic flow by appearing and disappearing. It is a useful way to change the environment as the play develops and moves along without any visual human aid (cited in Idemudia, 2012, p. 157). The scenic specification changes and adopts a different scenic appearance in each performance space as the performance develops and moves, resulting in a multi-transitional space that adopts numerous scenic looks concurrently (Idemudia, 2012, p. 157). Because of this, the directorial function in an African traditional performance can be fluid and adaptable, just like the nature of the performance itself.

Chapter 13

Blocking and Movement

This chapter deals extensively with blocking and movement, particularly because a good knowledge and understanding of the dynamics of blocking and movement in directorial art will aid directors in their use of movement or when blocking for the stage, film or television. This chapter shall review Erik Sean McGiven's article "Blocking and Movement." Blocking, as already defined in chapter three, is the rational positioning and movement of characters and objects to tell a story in visual terms on the stage space. McGiven claims that this arrangement or positioning might reflect the attitudes of characters toward one another, allowing the audience to understand the plot situation with or without words. Blocking helps viewers perceive the subtextual meaning among and between characters, even when it contradicts the conversation (n.d.). He adds that blocking should reflect the moment-to-moment failure or success of each character's struggle towards their objective, as well as the intensity (commitment) and focus (direction) of their emotions. In his words:

> Blocking is the accumulation of several components: the dramatic relationship of characters, their wants, what they feel, the obstacles on their way, and how the conflict is presently resolving. In this sense, it does not really matter whether the characters achieve their goal(s), but whether they are succeeding or failing at specific moments, in course of the dramatic action (McGiven, n.d.).

Blocking, therefore, is a holistic portrayal of strong and weak movements and relative positions on stage. The implication here is that certain body positions, stage areas, planes, and levels, as well as character movements, have definite values because they infuse meaning into the picture and the telling of a story.

Movement and Physical Behaviour of Characters

Movement on stage has varying degrees of meaning in relation to the type, body position and stage area of the actor at the time of executing the movement. A strong movement of a figure, as defined by McGiven (n.d.), is one that involves rising from a chair, straightening up, placing weight on the forward foot, raising the arm, or walking forward. Stepping backwards, slouching, putting weight on the back foot, sitting down, lowering the arm, walking backwards, turning around, or going away from a figure or object, on the other hand, are weak movements. Physical behaviours of actors on stage can also be defined in terms of whether they are strong or weak, whether they signify a winning attitude or one of struggle or failure. McGiven (n.d.) identified the following behavioural dispositions of actors in the theatre in relation to movement:

Strong, Winning Attitudes: Confident, direct, controlled, definite goals or wants, aggressive, assertive, strong speech patterns, concise movement, firm, stand ground, good self-image, relaxed, dominant, independent, resilient, self-sufficient, wanting something, control over life's choices, emotions open, changing for better, growing, sincere and many others.

Weak, Struggling or Failing Attitudes: Uncertain, lacking confidence, hesitant, not in control, reactionary, unsure or second thoughts about goals, emotionally tense, submissive, intimidated, evasive eyes, suffering in pain, masking or hiding emotions, giving ground-retreating, reliant, needing something, indecisive, fragile, regressive, little or no control over life's choices and many others.

Stage Orientations and Emphasis

This section discusses stage areas, planes, levels, and their relative strengths. The stage is divided into various areas and judged from the actor's perspective facing the audience.

Figure 13.1: Stage Areas

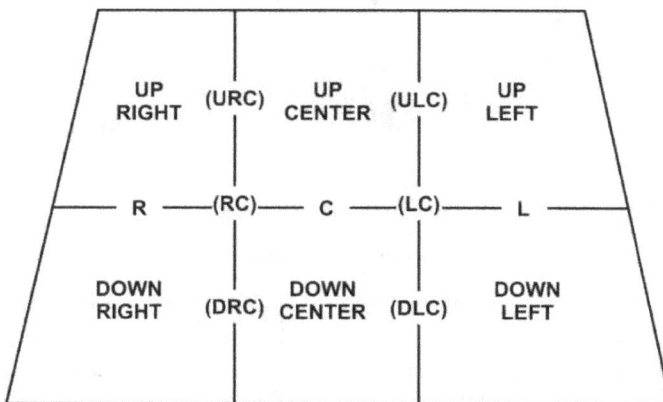

Source: Mark, 2023

According to McGiven (n.d.), in major opera productions, the back portion of the sloped stage is elevated to allow a better perspective of the company. This is how the names "upstage" and "downstage" came to be. As seen in the image above, the rest of the stage is divided into up right centre, down left centre, and so on. The movement on the stage from or to other places indicates its relative strength. The following chart provides the value of lines of movements of a moving figure not only in strong and weak stage movements, but also in the relative degree of strength and weakness of the stage area. Movements that are indicated by the number (1) are strongest in each set.

Figure 13.2: Charts Showing Strengths of Movements

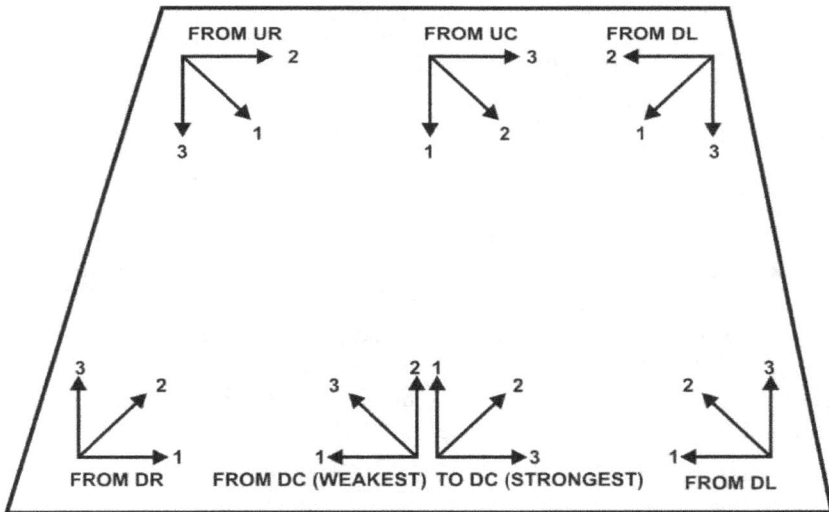

Source: Mark, 2023

McGiven (n.d.) points out that when a strong stage movement is followed by a weak body movement, the stage movement becomes weak. For instance, unless the figure performs a strong body movement after sitting, the overall effect is weak if they shift from upstage to downstage centre. Similar to this, a weak stage movement followed by a strong body movement can be strengthened. For instance, a dramatic and emphatic exit can be achieved by advancing from downstage to upstage and turning full front for a character's final line of dialogue before exiting the stage. McGiven (n.d.) contends in a similar vein that a transition from a weaker to a stronger area is a strong movement as such; crucial dialogue and stage business can be strengthened, adding emphasis to the character. A character who is held in a weak stage area until the essential moment, on the other hand, will get stronger when moving from a weak to a strong area; in fact, they will get stronger than if they stayed in the strong area continuously. This idea of relative strength and weakness holds true in many aspects of blocking.

The same relativity principle applies in terms of movement strength regarding the various planes and levels of the stage. The planes, according to McGiven (n.d.), are parts of the stage drawn parallel to the footlights. They are as long as the scenery opening and as wide as the actor standing in the plane. When all other criteria are equal, such as body position, level, and distance left or right of centre, the figure downstage or at the front (close to the audience) is stronger than the character upstage or near the back wall. As a character moves upstage, his strength diminishes proportionally. He also mentions levels as the elevation of the actor above the stage floor. The weakest may be lying on the floor, followed by sitting on the floor, then sitting on a chair, sitting on a chair's arm, standing, standing on one step, two stairs, and so on until the actor reaches the top of a stairway or a high platform. Generally, the higher the level of the character, the stronger his position (McGiven, n.d.).

There are exceptions where contrasting positions or lighting come into play. The attention of the audience is attracted by anything that is out of the norm. An example of this would be an actor sitting in an armchair while the rest of the group is standing. Another example is where a group on a platform is in shadows and to the side, while one character stands at stage level in a well-lit area. A third exception is where sightlines of the group at various levels are directed on a character at mid-elevation (McGiven, n.d.).

Body Positions

There are eight basic body positions from the perspective of the actor facing the audience or the camera. In the Full Front, as noted by McGiven, the actor faces the audience or camera and is seen as being in the strongest of the body positions. Open (strong) positions are those that are Full Front, One-Quarter Right (slightly inclined to the right), and One-Quarter Left (slightly slanted to the left). The actor generally stands in a Full Back position for a short while, with his back to the camera or audience. This body position, which is the weakest of the eight, is typically employed for dramatic effect (McGiven, n.d.).

The Three Quarter Right position has the actor almost facing back, slightly angled towards stage left. It is achieved by turning anti-clockwise from Full Front. The Three Quarter Left position has the actor almost facing back, slightly angled towards stage right. It is achieved by turning clockwise from Full Front. These two body positions are weak body positions. When an actor stands or sits facing either to the left or right, allowing the camera or audience to see only one side of the face and body, it is called the Profile Position. In the Profile Right position, the actor turns 90 degrees right, facing stage right; the left side of the face faces the audience. In the Profile Left position, the actor turns 90 degrees left, facing stage left; the right side of the face faces the audience. When two actors face one another in profile, they are said to be 'sharing' the scene. Also referred to as the half position, this body position is not particularly strong. In theatre, the actor looking to his right is said to be in 'right profile' and the left side of the face and body is open to the audience, while the actor looking to his left is said to be in 'left profile', and the right side of the face and body is open to the audience. For the camera actor, facing to the right is actually the same as a camera's left profile. This is because all positions for the screen actor are designated from the camera's point of view (McGiven, n.d.).

Figure 13.3: Theatre Body Positions

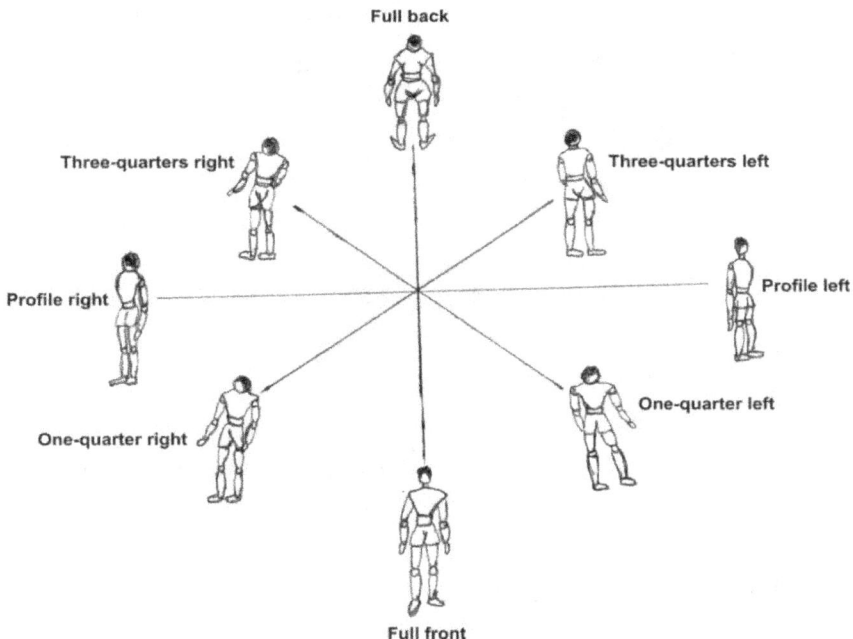

Full back

Three-quarters right

Three-quarters left

Profile right

Profile left

One-quarter right

One-quarter left

Full front

Source: Mark, 2023

Blocking Positions

Blocking positions, according to McGiven (n.d.), are where the characters are situated in respect to one another and the audience. As was already said, each position has a strong or weak value and presents chances to highlight particular dramatic aspects of the characters, their relationships, and the plot. Two characters will be utilized in the examples to help illustrate the fundamental concepts of blocking positions. Importantly, as new characters are introduced to a scene, blocking positions are frequently decided by a character's relationship to the character dominating the story at that moment.

Figure 13.4: Theatre Blocking Positions

These blocking positions can be modified by using the one-quarter front position or the three-quarter back position. Below are some of these variations:

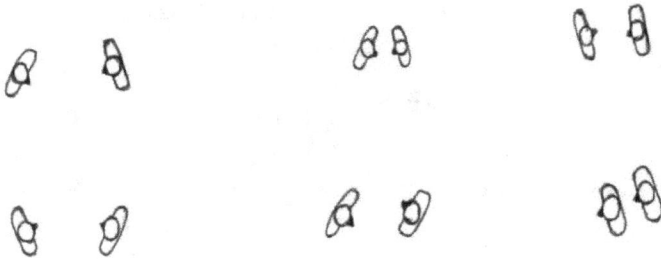

Other Blocking Positions: (weaker - sometimes theatrical)

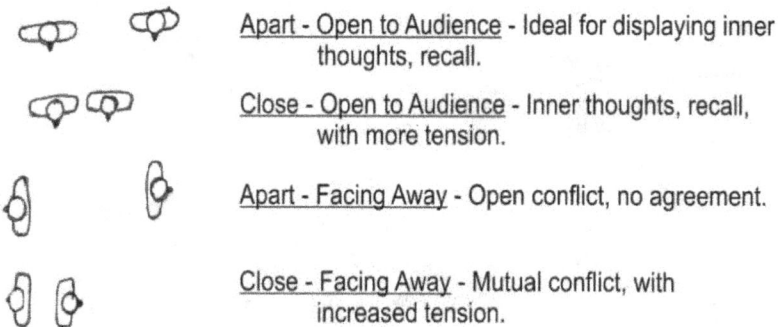

Apart - Open to Audience - Ideal for displaying inner thoughts, recall.

Close - Open to Audience - Inner thoughts, recall, with more tension.

Apart - Facing Away - Open conflict, no agreement.

Close - Facing Away - Mutual conflict, with increased tension.

Source: Mark, 2023

Figure 13.5: Blocking Positions

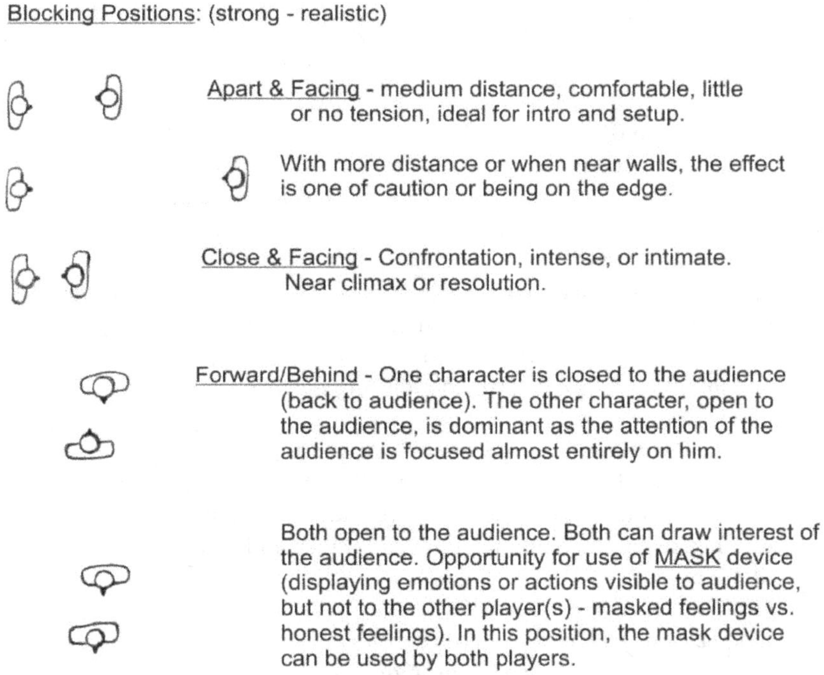

Blocking Positions: (strong - realistic)

Apart & Facing - medium distance, comfortable, little
or no tension, ideal for intro and setup.

With more distance or when near walls, the effect
is one of caution or being on the edge.

Close & Facing - Confrontation, intense, or intimate.
Near climax or resolution.

Forward/Behind - One character is closed to the audience
(back to audience). The other character, open to
the audience, is dominant as the attention of the
audience is focused almost entirely on him.

Both open to the audience. Both can draw interest of
the audience. Opportunity for use of MASK device
(displaying emotions or actions visible to audience,
but not to the other player(s) - masked feelings vs.
honest feelings). In this position, the mask device
can be used by both players.

Source: Mark, 2023

Acknowledgement and Support

According to McGiven (n.d.), once the characters and their relationships have been defined, the performers must acknowledge and support these decisions in order for the scene's goal to be best depicted. The scenario will be unclear to the audience if the actors are not in sync with one another or wander off in different dramatic directions. As an example, suppose the world's strongest man walks in and you shake his hand. We have two persons shaking hands with no assistance. But by 'feeling' the pain of his firm handshake, the character of the world's strongest man comes to life. And the strongest man does not need to do anything out of the ordinary. He does not have to put up a brave face. He is powerful, and your reaction confirms this. Another example is when two persons await the coming of a dignitary, a person of great importance. What is the significance? The actors, by their blocking and physical behaviour, can highlight this relationship through acknowledgement and support. The dignitary enters, and another party makes introductions.

That is the action, and if you understand the relationship, you can block the scene to reflect this.

The following are variations in status depicted by blocking and physical behaviour:

Considerable difference in Status: Two servants, new to a place, are being introduced to the queen as she makes her rounds. A humble bow or curtsy by the servants standing in place is acknowledged by a quick nod from the queen. Then she continues on her way.

Moderate difference in Status: The Prime Minister is being introduced to two local officials. The two officials would stand at the same time, then one by one, would come forward to shake hands with the Prime Minister, then return directly to their original places.

Very Little difference in Status: A new company executive is being introduced to his two staff members. The staff members would stand and move to the executive, with one leading the way. They would, in turn, shake hands, remain comfortably close and go into conversation (McGiven, n.d.).

Blocking can be used to accentuate certain aspects of a story. When there are several persons on the stage, the audience's attention is split among the characters. As performers and directors, it is your obligation to direct this focus to the appropriate person. How is this accomplished? When you watch a play or a movie, your eyes are drawn to the places with the most activity and away from the areas with less action. Close-ups focus our attention to the eyes and, when the character is speaking, occasionally to the mouth. These are regions where there is movement. Similarly, the audience's attention will be pulled to the person with the most significant action in the scene.

The sightlines of the characters help to direct the audience's attention. We have a habit of seeking in the same places that others do. On the other hand, our eyes are easily satisfied by redundant behaviour (such as someone looking at another person). Our eyes seek excitement or the possibility of excitement, such as a person doing, speaking, reacting, experiencing, thinking, or about to act. This potential for excitement is sometimes what creates suspense, and directors must know when and how to focus the audience's attention to vital stage events, characters, and objects.

For McGiven (n.d), the tension in a scene is very much a function of blocking. Some think of tension as being a lot of frantic motion or the unleashing of big emotions. Tension is actually the opposite. It is the restriction or confinement of motion or emotions. Tension is strongest when we sense the power behind some impending action. Once the action takes place and the power is unleashed, the tension decreases. Tension is like that of a rubber band being stretched to the breaking point or like that of a bomb with a lit fuse. To create tension, directors should look for the dramatic forces in a scene, and then confine them. You can maintain this tension by delaying or repressing the inevitable.

Implementing Choices

Blocking and movement must emanate from the character, whether it is motivated by a need, desire, or drive. Due to this, when blocking a scene, directions should be carried out in terms of motive and objective, such as to better observe, grab something, be close to something, stretch, and so forth. Instead of offering arbitrary instructions to cross from R to L and other such movements, blocking positions and movement are justified in this way by describing the impulse behind it. Of course, there will be instances where the movement and blocking of one or more characters is done to prepare for a particular scene interaction. According to McGiven (n.d.), the actor and director may need to decide on and start the motivation for such acts in certain situations.

During the run-through and rehearsal periods, the blocking evolves as the characters come to life. Most actors write notations in the script as the blocking directions. These might be either shorthand symbols or graphic depictions of the moves and positions. It is a good idea to write these down with a soft lead pencil, as most will be modified as the rehearsal progresses. You should also include your motivation for key moves and physical behaviours. In a long play or film shoot, such notations can greatly improve the clarity and continuity of the overall performance (McGiven, n.d.).

As actors, hitting your mark or being at your best in terms of character portrayal may seem difficult at first, but by walking through it a number of times, the body somehow remembers. It will, with practice, become a conditioned response. This is a skill one should work on by using a variety of methods. Some marks are relative to furniture, others to characters, and some even to the camera's location. Practise various actions, movements, and even dialogue and attempt to hit your mark on a specific word or action. In film, hitting your mark becomes crucial because the camera location, lighting, and sometimes special effects are based on your being at a certain position at a given time. You can't cheat because the camera will catch you looking for your mark. Your skill in this area improves with practice and actual experience, especially when you rely most on your body's ability to remember (McGiven, n.d.). According to McGiven (n.d.), there are techniques to give movement to two characters who are in stationary poses, such as standing or sitting, even if they are facing one another. The posture of the actor(s) may need to be adjusted, as well as minor movements like head rotations and lookaways. You can use your behaviour as actors to make a statement. Each of these actions can add context to the scene: leaning in, turning away, crossing one's knees, folding one's arms. The character's internal conflict can be more powerfully conveyed through the articulated desire to stand or flee than through the actual action. This sparks the interest of the spectator in the conflict's resolution.

McGiven (n.d) also opines that blocking, like dialogue, comes out of the character, his/her relationships, wants, feelings, and the obstacles he/she faces. It can be made emphatic when isolated from other dramatic elements. You can notice that by moving and speaking at the same time, each element diminishes, drowns or overshadows the other. On the other hand, if we isolate every move from the dialogue, we lose the impact of contrast and variety. Thus, the decision to isolate certain blocking moves; must come out of the characters and the story they live.

Stage versus Screen Blocking

In the theatre, the actor is required to reach out with his character and move the audience. In screen acting, the audience, because of the intimacy of the big screen, comes to the actor. The screen actor must underplay and do less, especially in close-ups. Another difference is that on the stage, there is more space between the characters, and total body behaviour is more dominant. On the screen, action has to be tightly blocked to allow the camera to capture the dominating behaviour of the characters' faces (McGiven, n.d.). Theatre actors tend to favour open-body positions rather than closed. This allows the audience to read the faces of the players. In film, the character's moves, blocking, and body positions are more realistic as there is no imaginary forth wall, and the camera can be moved to almost any angle. Such moves are motivated by the audience's desire (via the director and editor) to get a better perspective and to obtain more information. Some camera angles give into this desire while others delay or suspend it (McGiven, n.d.).

Because the stage picture is spread to give good balance and composition, the stage actor makes horizontal crosses more than vertical ones. In film, we think more in terms of depth rather than width, as the camera can pan or be repositioned from numerous vantage points. The screen, likewise, can isolate action or, with cuts, parts of an action. Thus, matching gestures, moves, and dialogue from a long shot to a closer angle becomes a critical concern for the screen actor. This attention to continuity is also important in repeated takes from the same angle (McGiven, n.d.). On the stage, the actor is required to extend moves and gestures to reach the last row of the people seated in the theatre. On the other hand, the screen actor must reduce body actions, understate his performance, and allow the camera to carry the performance to the viewers. The Falseness of the performance is more apparent in screen acting as big-screen close-ups reveal the slightest insincerity. Good screen performances require a life-like naturalness and the ability to do less without energy loss. In spite of the minor differences, the blocking principles remain consistent for both mediums (McGiven, n.d.).

At times, an actor, through his own nervousness or ineptness, will make unnecessary and distracting movements. These movements continue to bring attention to the actor, resulting in ambiguous character behaviour that leads the audience away from the story. Another fault is attempting to act on too many facets of the character at the same time. The definition and importance of the character are thus diminished, and the audience will care little and root less (McGiven, n.d.). The most important quality for a talented actor or director is arguably the ability to make firm, unwavering decisions and to stick with them. You must keep everything simple in terms of your choices for physical behaviour, blocking, and movement in order for the audience to comprehend the character's actions and how they relate to the plot as it develops.

In conclusion, McGiven (n.d.) believes that the director's role is to guarantee that the actor performs the character genuinely so that the context of the scene appears realistic and believable. To accomplish this, the actor must travel physically and psychologically through the same tale as the other actors. This entails considering the essentials of drama - the conflicting goals, the emotions, the failing and winning aspects of the struggle - all of which must rise to the surface, all of which must be seen, heard and felt. If you accomplish this, the play will have meaning. It will have a pattern, a dramatic shape, and, most importantly, it will have the desired effect on the audience.

Chapter 14

Directorial Concept and Directorial Approach

Directorial Concept

The word concept means an abstract idea. It refers to an idea that has been conceived in the human mind, in this sense, the mind of the director. This concept exists only in the thoughts of the director, having no concrete or physical appearance or form. The director then goes on to give this abstract idea a physical form or representation when he picks up a play and creatively interprets it on stage before an audience, using the stage production as a conduit or channel to pass his message/idea to the audience through sounds and pictures. A directorial concept is an abstract idea that a director has conceived and intends to transmit to the audience through a stage interpretation of a play. It is the message the director wants to pass to the audience, and this message or vision is what binds all aspects of the entire production together. Consequently, all members of the creative team work in unity to the realization of this goal. It may as well mean the director's vision of how the play is going to be performed or his image of the production. It is the central idea of unifying all elements of the production to make it unique. Hence, a directorial concept is a director's intended message for the spectators or society, which he aims to pass through his play interpretation.

In passing this message (signals) to the audience, the director uses transmitters, which Elam (1980) opines are, the bodies and voices of the actors, together with their metonymic accessories (costumes, properties etc.), elements of the set, electric lamps, musical instruments, tape recorders, film projectors and so on. The signals transmitted by these bodies are the movements, sounds and electrical impulses. These are all selected and arranged syntactically according to a wide range of signalling systems, which travel along a number of the physical channels available for human communication: from light and sound waves to olfactory and tactile means (p. 23). Hence, a directorial concept is a director's message for the audience as captured in his production.

In choosing a play, several factors influence a director's choice of script and having decided on the script; the director goes on to design every aspect of the production so that they reflect his intended message or concept for the production. The concept is the director's original invention, but its development and realization firmly lie in the hands of collaborators whose individual artistry and inclinations will invariably play a significant role in the form and impact of the outcome, according to Debra Bruch (1990). Therefore, the director's top priority is choosing trustworthy and qualified designers. A compromise that arises from this highly creative conversation is frequently better than the original vision since creative ideas interact with one another. When he meets with them, he shares his vision and listens to their suggestions. But in the end, the choice of the appropriate interpretation rests with the director.

Directional Approach

The director's chosen method of interpreting a play is known as the directorial approach. Two methods exist; presentational style and representational style. According to Daniel Kpodoh (2006), who cites Stanley Obuh, presentational is the theory and practice of drama as a frankly theoretical and fictional presentation, as opposed to the other extreme of representation, which aims to create the illusion of reality (p. 29). As a result, the representational technique entails a director interpreting a play realistically, as opposed to the presentational approach, which calls for a director to give a text an unrealistic interpretation.

Furthermore, Friedrich Dürrenmatt (1976) asserts that "the present-day theatre presents two aspects: on the one hand, a museum but the other, a field of experiments" (p. 59). This, therefore, means that we have two groups of directors: those who faithfully interpret a script as presented by the playwright and those who experiment with the script, going outside or beyond a playwright's idea. Johnson (2001), citing Oscar Brockett, identifies the first director as "one that faithfully or worshipfully interprets the work of the playwright as finely as possible, without adulterating it. The second is a director that uses theatrical elements, of which the script is merely one, to fashion his own artwork" (cited in Johnson, 2001, p. 122). This director, Brockett calls the "master artist" because he is able to recreate his own artwork from or outside the script and stamp his authority and style, which is different from that of the playwright.

The first director is a slavish director, more like a servant, who worships or venerates the script/playwright. Their regard for the script is so sacrosanct that they are unable to think outside or beyond or even do without the script. The second director is referred to as the heretic director or auteur director. This director has little or no regard for the script or text and can do without it. He only uses the script as a raw material and can rework the text to suit his preference, and the final product is uniquely his own. This group of directors strive to make a theatrical entity out of productions. They see the theatre as a field of experimental explorations. According to Brockett, the main distinction between the two is how they approach the script; in the second method, the director takes on many of the playwright's duties and transforms himself into a writer-adapter, molding the material (or having someone else mold it) in accordance with his conceptions. The two sorts of directors, however, have the same fundamental tools at their disposal and carry out the same fundamental duties while staging the script, regardless of how it was created (cited in Johnson, 2001, p. 122).

The complete understanding of the play that can be transferred into performance is what Kenneth Cameron and Theodore Hoffman (1974) refer to as the "directorial approach" (cited in Johnson, 2001, p. 123). This suggests that every director has a strategy that he or she employs to achieve the set goals of a production. For Cameron and Hoffman, cited in Johnson (2001, p.123), no one can show up to his first rehearsal or even his first casting session without having an approach. It does not have to be detailed in writing, but it may be; it also does not always have to be schematized in terms of character actions, blocking, and ground layouts. However, it must be able to be converted into a performance rather than just a verbal description. The director will, in a sense, have a clear vision of the play's artistic overarching goal (rather than just "what is it about" but "what will it do?").

Edwin Wilson (1991) argues that the notion of a directorial approach translates into the ability of a director to situate a production within the context of its historical ambit or other periods relevant to the play (cited in Johnson, 2001, p. 124). For example, if a director chooses to produce a play based on the Trojan War, he could do it in a typical Greek fashion or do it with reference to the Egba Wars or even the Civil War of Nigeria. The second type of approach a director can apply, as identified by Wilson, is where a director locates a central metaphor which represents and acts as a reference point, central to the overall maxim of the production. He cites the example of the production of *Hamlet* by William Shakespeare, where the metaphor of a "Spider's Web" is identified and strategically represented on the scenic design while actors express the "trapped" sense in every level until Hamlet is eventually caught by the web (cited in Johnson, 2001, p. 124).

A directorial approach must enhance the play's understanding and enjoyment by the audience in order for it to benefit the production. This position is supported by Brockett, cited in Johnson (2001, p.124), who opines that while innovations are desired and even enjoyed, every 'experiment' should be carried out in a way that theatre auditoriums are packed with enthusiastic audience members and not fizzling away of interest due to an experimental obsession that leaves much to be desired.

Conclusion

This book's goal is to give readers a comprehensive introduction to the practice of play directing. It looked at the director's history, characteristics, and resources in addition to theatrical and directing notions. It examined various types of directors, functions of the director, principles of directing and key theories and techniques of directing across Europe, West, South, North and East Africa. The concept and development of the theatre stage and the features, benefits, drawbacks, and implications of directing on the arena, proscenium, thrust, traverse, and African traditional theatre stage orientations have all been covered.

The study also looked at blocking and movement, the meaning of directorial concept and directorial approach, as well as their implications for directors. This book intends to provide both seasoned and aspiring directors with fundamental theatrical directing knowledge and direction on directing plays on various stage orientations.

List of References

Albright, H.D., William, H. and Lee, M, (1968). *Principles of theatre arts.* Boston, Houghton Mifflin.

Adedeji, J.A, (1981). 'Alaringo: The traditional Yoruba travelling theatre' in Ogunbiyi, Y (ed.) *Drama and theatre in Nigeria: A critical source book.* Lagos: Nigerian Magazine, pp. 221-248.

Adelugba, D, (1978). 'Wole Ogunyemi, Zulu Sofola and Ola Rotimi: Three dramatists in search of a language' in Ogunba, O. and Irele, A. (eds.) *Theatre in Africa.* Ibadan: University Press, pp. 201-220.

Adeoye, A. A, (2010). 'On theatre scholarship and controversy: The case of the director in the traditional African theatre'. *The African Symposium.* 10 (2), 84-93.

Adeoye, A.A, (2011). 'Directing styles in the Nigerian literary theatre.' *Journal of Performing Arts.* 4 (2), 32-42.

Adeoye, A.A, (2013). 'Two performances two worlds: Dapo Adelugba's directorial intervention in Soyinka's *kongi harvest* and Sotuminu's *the onion skin* considere'. *Ekpoma Journal of Theatre and Media Arts.* 4 (1-2), 1-15.

Agovi, K.E, (1991). 'Towards an authentic African theatre'. *Ufahamu.* 19 (2-3), 67-79.

Akyea, E.O, (1968). 'The Atwia-Ekumfi Kodzidan: An experimental African theatre'. *Okyeame.* 4 (1), 82-84.

Babalola, Y.S, (2017). 'The dynamics of directing for the stage and the screen'. *Ejotmas: Ekpoma Journal of Theatre and Media* Arts. 6 (1-2), 439-460.

Barranger, M, (1991). *Theatre: A way of seeing.* New York: Barnes & Noble Inc.

Baxter, V. and Aitchison, J, (2010). 'Embodying 'lightness' in the new South Africa – The theatre of Ellis Pearson and Bheki Mkhwane 1993-2008'. *South African Theatre Journal.* 24 (1), 51-66.

Bell-Gam, H. L, (2003). 'Akwafaribo: The directorial function of the master drummer in Nji-Owu performance of Opobo'. *Anyigba Journal of Arts and Humanities.* 2 (2), 9-15.

Bell-Gam, H.L, (2007). 'Rudiments of play directing' in Bell-Gam, H.L. (ed.) *Theatre in theory and practice for beginners.* Port Harcourt: University of Port Harcourt Press, pp. 71 -87.

Boukadida R, (2011). *Le Nouveau Théatre par lui-même. Entretiens avec Fadhel Jaibi, Mohamed Driss et Jalila Bac- car (1985-1987).* Tunis : Les Editions Sahar : Institut Su-perieur d'Art Dramatique.

Brockett, O. and Ball, R, (2013). *The essential theatre enhanced.* USA: Cengage Learning.

Bruch, D, (1990). 'Directing theatre'. Available at: http://www.danillitphil.com /base.html (Accessed: 12 January 2016).

Cameron, K. and Hoffman, T, (1974). *A guide to theatre studies 2nd edition.* New York: Macmillan Publishing Co. Inc.

Cash, J, (2014). 'Poor theatre conventions'. Available at: http://www.thedrama teacher.come/poor-theatre-conventions/ (Accessed: 1 February 2015).

Chatman, M, (2014). 'Types of stages'. Available at: https://prezi.com/7warqsiyidio /different-types-of-stages/ (Accessed: 5 February 2015).

Clurman, H, (1972). *On directing*. New York: The Macmillan Company.

Cohen, R, (2000). *Theatre* 5th ed. USA: Mayfield Publishing Company.

Cole, T. and Chinoy, K.H, (ed.) (1963). *Directors on directing*. USA: The BOBBS – MERIL Company, Inc.

Cook, D. A, (2014). *A history of narrative film*. New York: London, Norton.

Cremona, V.A, (2018). 'The poetics of confrontation: Fadhel Jaibi and the state in pre-revolutionary Tunisia'. *Nordic Theatre Studies*. 26(1), 68-79.

Dean, A. and Carra, L, (2009). *Fundamentals of play directing* 5th ed. U.S.A: Waveland Press Incorporated.

Downs, W. and Ramsey, W, (2012). *The art of theatre: A concise introduction*. Boston: Cengage Learning.

Durenmatt, F, (1976). *Writings on the theatre and drama*. London: Jonathan Cape Ltd.

Ebo, E. E, (2012). 'Traditional theatre architecture as a panacea for reviving live performance in Nigeria' in Ododo, S.E. (ed.) *Fireworks for a lighting aesthetician: Essays and tributes in honour of Duro Oni @ 60*. Lagos: Centre for Black and African Arts and Civilization, pp. 168- 176.

Ejiofor, B.A, (2007). 'Tenors of Classicism in theatre history' in Bell-Gam, H.L. (ed.) *Theatre in theory and practice for* beginners. Port Harcourt: University of Port Harcourt Press, pp. 2-20.

Elam, K, (1980). *The semiotics of theatre and drama*. London, Routledge.

Emasealu, E, (2010). *The theatre of Ola Rotimi: Production and performance dynamics*. Minna: Gurara Publishing.

Enendu, M, (2002). 'The development of performance venues and theatre architecture in Nigeria and implications on theatrical design' in Tokpbere, J. (ed.) *Design history in Nigeria*. Abuja: National Gallery of Arts, pp. 349-359.

Enita, O.G, (2008). 'Ukala, folkism and the laws of aesthetic response' in Asagba, A.O. (ed.) *Sam Ukala: His work at sixty*. Ibadan: Kraft Books Limited, pp. 48-57.

Frost, A. and Yarrow, R, (1990). *Improvisation in drama*. London: Macmillan International Higher Education.

George II, Duke of Saxe- Meiningen, (1963). 'Pictorial motion' in Cole, T. and Chinoy, H.K. (eds.) *Directors on directing*. USA: The BOBBS – MERIL Company Inc, pp. 81-88.

Grotowski, J, (1968). *Towards a poor theatre*. New York: Simon and Shuster.

Idemudia, E. U, (2012). 'Spaces in places of theatre performance' in Ododo, S.E. (ed.) *Fireworks for a lighting aesthetician: Essays and tributes in honour of Duro Oni @ 60*. Lagos: Centre for Black and African Arts and Civilization, pp. 155-167.

Innes, C. and Shetsova, M, (2013). *The Cambridge introduction to theatre directing*. Cambridge: Cambridge University Press.

Irisoanga, C, (2000). *Hand book of basic stage practice*. Port Harcourt: Oroki Press.

Johnson, E, (2001). *Play production processes*. Lagos: Concept Publications Limited.

Johnson, E, (2003). *Visions towards a mission: The art of interpretative directing*. Lagos: Concept Publication Limited.

Kahuro, K, (2018). *The art of stage directing: A case of three Kenyan directors*. Master's thesis. Kenyatta University, pp.1-135.

Kpodoh, D.O, (2006). Directing in an educational theatre: A case study of Bakare Ojo Rasaki's *drums of war*. Unpublished bachelor's thesis. University of Port Harcourt.

Krama, C, (2006). *African traditional theatre and drama: Themes and perspectives*. Port Harcourt: University of Port Harcourt Press.

Lawal, H. O, (2010). *Fundamentals of theatre arts*. Ibadan: Glory-land Publishing Company.

Mark, G. T, (2015). Directing in contemporary Nigerian theatre: A stage production of Ahmed Yerima's *hard ground*. Unpublished master's thesis. University of Port Harcourt.

Mark, G.T, (2023). *Circular formation* [Photograph]. Port Harcourt: Mark Gasper Tekena.

Mark, G.T, (2023). *Zig-zag formation* [Photograph]. Port Harcourt: Mark Gasper Tekena.

Mark, G.T, (2023). *Serpentine formation* [Photograph]. Port Harcourt: Mark Gasper Tekena.

Mark, G.T, (2023). *The straight line formation* [Photograph]. Port Harcourt: Mark Gasper Tekena.

Mark, G.T, (2023). *Curve formation* [Photograph]. Port Harcourt: Mark Gasper Tekena.

Mark, G.T, (2023). *Arc formation* [Photograph]. Port Harcourt: Mark Gasper Tekena.

Mark, G.T, (2023). *Angular formations* [Photograph]. Port Harcourt: Mark Gasper Tekena.

Mark, G.T, (2023). *Square formation* [Photograph]. Port Harcourt: Mark Gasper Tekena.

Mark, G.T, (2023). *Diagonal formation* [Photograph]. Port Harcourt: Mark Gasper Tekena.

Mark, G.T, (2023). *Levels of movement* [Photograph]. Port Harcourt: Mark Gasper Tekena.

Mark, G.T, (2023). *Directions of movement* [Photograph]. Port Harcourt: Mark Gasper Tekena.

Mark, G.T, (2023). *The Greek theatre* [Photograph]. Port Harcourt: Mark Gasper Tekena.

Mark, G.T, (2023). *Roman theatre* [Photograph]. Port Harcourt: Mark Gasper Tekena.

Mark, G.T, (2023). *The medieval stage* [Photograph]. Port Harcourt: Mark Gasper Tekena.

Mark, G.T, (2023). *The elizabethan theatre* [Photograph]. Port Harcourt: Mark Gasper Tekena.

Mark, G.T, (2023). *The restoration stage* [Photograph]. Port Harcourt: Mark Gasper Tekena.

Mark, G.T, (2023). *The proscenium theatre* [Photograph]. Port Harcourt: Mark Gasper Tekena.

Mark, G.T, (2023). *The arena stage* [Photograph]. Port Harcourt: Mark Gasper Tekena.

Mark, G.T, (2023). *The proscenium stage* [Photograph]. Port Harcourt: Mark Gasper Tekena.

Mark, G.T, (2023). *The proscenium stage positions* [Photograph]. Port Harcourt: Mark Gasper Tekena.

Mark, G.T, (2023). *Horizontal movements* [Photograph]. Port Harcourt: Mark Gasper Tekena.

Mark, G.T, (2023). *Curved movements* [Photograph]. Port Harcourt: Mark Gasper Tekena.

Mark, G.T, (2023). *Vertical movements* [Photograph]. Port Harcourt: Mark Gasper Tekena.

Mark, G.T, (2023). *Diagonal crossing movements* [Photograph]. Port Harcourt: Mark Gasper Tekena.

Mark, G.T, (2023). *Angular movements* [Photograph]. Port Harcourt: Mark Gasper Tekena.

Mark, G.T, (2023). *The thrust stage* [Photograph]. Port Harcourt: Mark Gasper Tekena.

Mark, G.T, (2023). *The traverse stage* [Photograph]. Port Harcourt: Mark Gasper Tekena.

Mark, G.T, (2023). *Ekuechi facekuerade performance stage* [Photograph]. Port Harcourt: Mark Gasper Tekena.

Mark, G.T, (2023). *Procession and staging of Ekuechi facekuerade performance* [Photograph]. Port Harcourt: Mark Gasper Tekena.

Mark, G.T, (2023). *Stage areas* [Photograph]. Port Harcourt: Mark Gasper Tekena.

Mark, G.T, (2023). *Charts showing strengths of movements* [Photograph]. Port Harcourt: Mark Gasper Tekena.

Mark, G.T, (2023). *Theatre body positions* [Photograph]. Port Harcourt: Mark Gasper Tekena.

Mark, G.T, (2023). *Theatre blocking positions* [Photograph]. Port Harcourt: Mark Gasper Tekena.

Mark, G.T, (2023). *Blocking positions* [Photograph]. Port Harcourt: Mark Gasper Tekena.

Mcgiven, E.S, (n.d.). 'Blocking and movement'. Available at: http://www.eric seanmcgiven.com/writings/acting/blocking-and-movement/ (Accessed 23 June 2016).

Mendenhall, M, (2017). 'Advantages of the thrust stage'. Available at: https:// ourpastimes.com/advantages-of-the-thrust-stage-12544768.html (Accessed 23 June 2016).

Moore, S, (1984). *The Stanislavski system*. New York: NY Penguin.

Murray, S. and Keefe, J, (2007). *Physical theatres: A critical introduction*. London and New York: Routledge,

Musa, R, (2006). 'Talking with the master, rethinking play directing: An interview with Ziky Kofoworola'. *The Performer: Ilorin Journal of the Performing Arts*. 8, 1-11.

Nnenyelike, N, (2010). 'The director as a theatre critic: The case of Dapo Adelugba'. *Creative Artist: A Journal of Theatre and Media Studies*. 4 (1), 145-164.

Nnenyelike, N, (2011). 'A stage director must adopt production style - Dr. Adeoye'. Available at: http://www.vanguardngr.com/2011/04a-stage-director-must-adopt-production-style-dr- adeoye (Accessed 2 January 2016).

Ododo, S.E, (2009). 'The playing aesthetics of Ebiran Ekuechi facekuerade festival'. *Perfformio: Journal of the Performing Arts*. 1 (1), 28-45.

Ododo, S.E, (2015). *Facekuerade theatre: A performance model from Ebira-Ekuechi*. Maiduguri: Society of Nigeria Theatre Artists (SONTA).

Oga, C. E, (2007). 'Theatre directing: An introductory statement' in Bell-Gam, H.L. (ed.) *Theatre in theory and practice for beginners*. Port Harcourt: University of Port Harcourt Press, pp. 88-95.

Ogunbiyi, Y, (1981). 'Nigerian theatre and drama: A critical profile' in Ogunbiyi, Y. (ed.) *Drama and theatre in Nigeria: A critical source book*. Lagos: Nigerian Magazine, pp. 3-51.

Ogunkilede.J, (1987). *Theatre technology in Jimoh Alieu cultural organization*. Calabar: Tha. Arts.

Ogunyele, F, (2008). 'Ori Olokun theatre and the town and gown policy' in Banham, M., James, G. and Osofisan, F. (eds.) *African theatre companies*. USA: Boydell & Brewer Inc, pp. 16-26.

Osofisan, F, (1986). 'The place of theatre in the cultural development of Nigeria' in Unoh, S.O. (ed.) *Cultural development and nation building*. Ibadan: Spectrum, pp.41-51.

Pickering, J.V, (1981). *Theatre: A contemporary introduction* 3rd ed. USA: West Publishing Co.

Britannica, (n.d.). 'Proscenium theatre'. Available at: http://www.britannica.com/art/proscenium (Accessed 10 July 2015).

Raja, G, (2017). 'A matter of thrust: Directing for the jagriti stage'. Available at: https://www.jagrititheatre.com/blog/a-matter-of-thrust-directing-for-the-jagriti- stage/ (Accessed 5 February 2015).

Rotimi, O, (1983). *If: a tragedy of the ruled*. Ibadan: Heinemann Educational Books (Nigeria) Plc.

Stanislavski, K, (1963). 'Creative work with the actor' in Cole, T. and Chinoy, H.K. (eds.) *Directors on directing*. USA: The BOBBS – MERIL Company Inc, pp. 109-118.

Sutherland, F, (1961). 'Venture into theatre'. *Okyeame*. 1(1),47-48.

Sutherland, F, (1987). *The marriage of Anansewa*. UK: Longman Group Limited.

Trumbull, E. W, (2008). 'Introduction to theatre online course: The director'. Available at: http://novaonline.nvcc.edu/eli/spd130et/director.htm (Accessed 12 January 2016).

Twijnstra, R. and Durden, E, (2014). *Theatre directing in South Africa*. South Africa: Jacana Media.

Anglistik, (n.d.). 'Types of Stages'. Available at: http://www2.anglistik.uni-freiburg.de/intranet/englishbasics/DramaTypesofStages01.htm (Accessed 10 July 2015).

Ukala, S, (1990). *Akpakaland in five plays*. Ibadan: H.E.B.

Ukala, S, (1977). *The placenta of death in two plays*. Agbor: Oris Press.

Ukala, S, (1996). 'Folkism: Towards a national aesthetic principle for Nigerian dramaturgy'. *New Theatre Quarterly*. 12 (47), 279 – 287.

Ukala, S, (2000). 'Rotimi, tradition and his audience' in Emenyonu, E. (ed.) *Goatskin bags and wisdom: New critical perspectives on African literature*. Trenton, N.J: Africa World Press Inc, pp. 91-104.

Uwatt, B.E, (2002). 'Ola Rotimi's impact on playwriting and directing in Nigeria' in Uwatt, E.B. (ed.) *Playwriting and directing in Nigeria: Interviews with Ola Rotimi*. Lagos: Apex Books Limited, pp.1-17.

Vaux, R, (2017). 'Types of theatre rehearsals'. Available at: https://ourpastimes.com/types-of-theater-rehearsals-12543089.html (Accessed 20 January 2018).

Vertesi, C, (2017). 'What is traverse staging?' Available at: https://ourpastimes.com/what-is-traverse-staging-12169441.html (Accessed 10 July 2015).

Wainstein, M, (2012). *Stage directing: A director's itinery*. Indianpolis, USA: Harckett Publishing Company.

Wills, R, (ed.) (1976). *The director in a changing theatre*. California: Mayfield Publishing.

Wilson, E, (2004). *The theatre experience* 9th ed. New Year: McGraw-Hill.

Yerima, A, (2006). *Hard ground*. Ibadan: Kraft Books Limited.

About the Author

Tekena Gasper Mark is a poet, novelist, director and dramatist with research interests in African Theatre, Film and Performance Studies. He teaches in the Department of Theatre and Film Studies, Rivers State University, Port Harcourt, Nigeria, with over seven years of experience as a researcher and lecturer. His book *Ideas on Directing Experimental Theatre* (Nigeria, 2016) provides insights on the practice of experimental theatre directors and theorists such as Erwin Piscator and Bertolt Brecht, Vsevolod Meyerhold, Antonin Artaud, Jerzy Grotowski, Martin Esslin, Augusto Boal and two Nigerian theatre directors— Felix Okolo and Segun Adefila. He holds a Ph.D in play directing and teaches directing, playwriting, dramatic theory and criticism, and music theatre.

Index

A

AbdulRasheed Abiodun Adeoye, 55
action, 4, 5, 11, 12, 14, 16, 19, 29, 31, 34, 35, 36, 37, 42, 43, 49, 50, 51, 58, 59, 60, 66, 67, 68, 71, 73, 78, 81, 82, 83, 85, 87, 88, 89, 91, 93, 94, 95, 98, 102, 111, 118, 119, 120
Africa, xiv, 3, 45, 63, 101, 106, 127, 129, 134
African Traditional Theatre, 4, 101, 105, 106
Ahmed Yerima, 20, 21, 23, 131
Akwafaribo, 106, 107, 108, 129
Alexander Dean, 19
Anansegoro, xiv, 59, 60, 61
Anansesem, 59, 60
Andre Antoine, 2, 8, 9
anti-realistic theatre, 9
approaches, 4, 14, 16, 31, 73
apron stage, 76
Aquatic Theatre, xiv, 52, 53
Arena Stage, 81, 82, 83, 103
Arundhati Raja, 95
audience, 1, 2, 4, 10, 11, 14, 15, 16, 19, 21, 29, 31, 32, 34, 35, 37, 38, 41, 42, 43, 44, 45, 46, 47, 48, 49, 51, 52, 53, 55, 57, 59, 60, 61, 65, 67, 68, 69, 70, 71, 72, 73, 75, 76, 77, 78, 81, 82, 83, 84, 85, 86, 87, 88, 89, 91, 93, 94, 95, 96, 97, 98, 99, 101, 102, 103, 104, 107, 110, 111, 112, 114, 115, 116, 117, 118, 120, 121, 123, 125, 134
aural aesthetics, 19
Auteur director, 12

Avenue Stage, 103

B

Babalola, 19, 129
balance, 19, 70, 96, 120
beauty, 9, 19, 107
Bertolt Brecht, 13, 135
Bheki Mkhwane, xiv, 63, 64, 67, 129
blocking, xv, 3, 4, 5, 7, 15, 16, 17, 22, 23, 67, 84, 87, 89, 91, 94, 96, 98, 108, 111, 114, 116, 117, 118, 119, 120, 121, 125, 127, 132
Blocking and Movement, 111
body positions, xv, 16, 19, 111, 114, 120, 132

C

Cameron and Gillespie, 14, 16
Cameron and Hoffman, 12, 125
casting, 14, 15, 50, 125
Chatman, 93, 130
Clurman, 7, 11, 14, 130
Cohen, 1, 7, 8, 9, 10, 130
Cole and Chinoy, 2, 8
Columbus Irisoanga, 27
composition, xiv, 16, 19, 20, 21, 24, 25, 26, 27, 45, 50, 52, 70, 120
Concept, 2, 5, 123, 131
Constantin Stanislavski, xiv, 8, 33, 34, 52
Contemporary Director, 7, 10
Convoluting Concourse of Variegated Happenings, xiv, 41
Cosmo-Humo Symbiosis, xiv, 58

D

Dapo Adelugba, xiv, 41, 51, 52, 129, 133
David Belasco, 9
David Cook, 13
Dean and Carra, 4, 19
Debra Bruch, 124
Didaskalos, 7
Dionysus, 2
Direct Emphasis, 19
directing, xiii, xiv, xv, 2, 3, 4, 7, 8, 9, 10, 13, 14, 19, 22, 31, 33, 41, 42, 44, 45, 52, 54, 55, 58, 70, 72, 73, 79, 83, 95, 102, 108, 127, 129, 130, 131, 133, 134, 135
directing styles, 8, 31, 70
directing theories, 31
Director, xiv, 4, 7, 11, 13, 16, 95
directorial approach, xv, 3, 41, 42, 56, 124, 125, 127
Diversified Emphasis, 19
drama, 1, 4, 9, 11, 12, 42, 49, 50, 52, 55, 63, 64, 70, 72, 73, 76, 102, 121, 124, 130, 131, 133
Duke of Saxe-Meiningen, xiv, 8, 31
Duo Emphasis, 19

E

Ebo, 101, 130
Edwin Wilson, 12, 125
Effiong Johnson, xiv, 54, 58
Ejiofor, v, 1, 130
Elizabethan stage, 75
Ellis Pearson, 63, 64, 67, 129
Emasealu, v, 4, 41, 44, 130
emphasis, xv, 19, 20, 34, 37, 39, 41, 44, 52, 113
Enendu Molinta, 110
Energy, 28, 29
Erik Sean McGiven, 111

Eugene Barbara, 13

F

Facekuerade Theatre, xiv, 56, 57
Fadhel Jaibi, xiv, 67, 68, 129, 130
Femi Osofisan, xiv, 41
Festival Theatre, xiv, 41
Flow, 28, 29
Fluid Stage, 103
Folkism, xiv, 45, 48, 49, 134
folkist theatre, 49, 51
folktale, 45, 46, 48, 49, 50, 51, 59
Force, 28, 29
French scenes, 17

G

George II, xiv, 8, 31, 32, 33, 130
gestures, 9, 13, 29, 33, 41, 43, 58, 71, 73, 95, 120
Given Circumstances, 34
Gordon Craig, 9, 53
Greek theatre, 85, 101, 131
Guatam Raja, 95

H

Hal Prince, 14
Hard Ground, 20, 21, 23
Harley Granville-Barker, 9
Henry Leopold Bell-Gam, v, xiv, 52
Heretical approach, 14
historical accuracy, 31

I

Idemudia, 109, 110, 130
Impact-Contact Aesthetics, xiv, 54
improvisational directing, 70, 72
Inih Akpan Ebong, xiv, 58

J

Jacques Copeau, 2
Jagriti theatre, 95
Jerzy Grotowski, xiv, 37, 135
Johnny Papp, 13
Johnson, 2, 4, 8, 12, 17, 54, 55, 58,
   59, 73, 82, 86, 93, 124, 125, 131
Joseph Chackin, 13
Joseph Murungu, xiv, 70, 72
Justin Cash, 37

K

Krama, v, 101, 102, 103, 104, 131

L

Lawal, 9, 31, 34, 131
Lawrence Carra, 19
laws of aesthetic response, 45, 130
Lee Strasberg, 37

M

Magic If, 34
Martha Mendenhall, 94
master metaphor, 14
Medieval Stage, 75
Method of Physical Action, 37
Micheal Chekhov, 37
Mild adapter director, 12
Milly Barranger, 13
mime, 29, 41, 44, 51, 63, 101, 104,
   108
mise-en-scène, 2, 37
modern directing, 7, 8
Moore, 36, 133
movement, xiv, xv, 3, 4, 5, 9, 13, 16,
   19, 21, 22, 23, 24, 25, 26, 27, 28,
   29, 31, 33, 44, 45, 53, 58, 61, 63,
   84, 94, 96, 104, 111, 112, 113,
   114, 118, 119, 121, 127, 131, 132
Movement Formations, 24
music, 1, 11, 19, 29, 31, 42, 44, 45,
   51, 53, 56, 57, 58, 59, 72, 104,
   108, 135

N

Neo-Alienation Aesthetics, xiv, 55
Nigerian traditional theatre stage,
   79
Nji-Owu performance, 106, 107,
   108, 129
Nneyelike, 51, 55, 56

O

objectives, xiv, 3, 4, 12, 36, 55, 71
Oga, 3, 11, 19, 20, 21, 29, 52, 133
Ola Rotimi, xiv, 4, 41, 42, 43, 44,
   47, 102, 106, 129, 130, 134
oratorical, 19
organic truth, 35
Orukoro, 54
Oscar Brockett, 12, 124
Otto Brahm, 9

P

pantomimic dramatization, xiv,
   19, 29
Paul Fort, 9
performances, 1, 4, 31, 34, 35, 41,
   42, 44, 46, 50, 51, 53, 57, 68, 75,
   76, 77, 79, 101, 103, 104, 105,
   106, 107, 108, 109, 110, 121, 129
performers, 1, 13, 16, 29, 34, 36,
   47, 48, 52, 53, 55, 57, 60, 67, 78,
   79, 83, 88, 89, 95, 98, 99, 103,
   105, 107, 108, 117, 118
Peter Brook, 11, 13, 66

Physical Theatre, xiv, 63
Pickering, 7, 133
picturization, xiv, 16, 19, 20, 52
play, 2, 3, 4, 5, 7, 9, 11, 12, 13, 14,
    15, 16, 17, 19, 20, 21, 29, 31, 33,
    34, 35, 36, 37, 38, 42, 45, 46, 48,
    49, 50, 51, 52, 53, 54, 56, 58, 59,
    61, 63, 64, 65, 67, 70, 71, 72, 73,
    77, 78, 81, 85, 88, 94, 95, 96, 97,
    98, 103, 110, 114, 118, 119, 121,
    123, 124, 125, 127, 129, 130, 133,
    135
playtext, 12
Poetics of Confrontation, xiv, 67
Poor Theatre, xiv, 37, 38
presentational approach, 124
Pressure Cooker, xiv, 41
principles of directing, xiv, 19, 127
production, 1, 2, 3, 8, 10, 11, 12,
    13, 14, 15, 16, 17, 20, 21, 23, 31,
    33, 37, 38, 42, 43, 51, 52, 53, 54,
    55, 58, 64, 69, 70, 71, 72, 79, 82,
    83, 94, 97, 123, 125, 131, 133
proscenium arch, 85, 86, 87, 88, 95
proscenium stage, xv, 3, 49, 78, 83,
    85, 86, 87, 88, 93, 132

R

Realistic Directors, 7
rehearsal, 13, 15, 31, 37, 42, 51, 54,
    65, 108, 119, 125
rhythm, xiv, 11, 16, 19, 29, 43, 57,
    58, 69, 71, 108
Richard Schechner, 13
rituals, 1, 53, 79, 101
Robert Cohen, 2
Robert Wills, 2
Roman theatre, 131

S

Sam Ukala, xiv, xv, 45, 46, 48, 130
Scene, 21, 23, 66
screen acting, 120, 121
Secondary Emphasis, 19
sequence, 19, 20, 29, 35, 37, 58, 61,
    108
Shoreline Stage, 103
slavish director, 12, 124
song, 19, 23, 44, 46, 51, 55, 60, 61,
    104, 108
sound and effect, 19
Space, 28, 29, 57, 58
speech, 19, 29, 31, 44, 51, 52, 69,
    71, 95, 99, 112
stability, 19
Stage, 4, 22, 23, 56, 73, 75, 76, 77,
    78, 79, 89, 90, 91, 101, 103, 105,
    106, 112, 120, 132, 134
Stage areas, 132
Stanley Obuh, 124
Stella Adler, 33, 37
Stylizing Directors, 7
Sunday Enessi Ododo, xiv, 56
super-objective, 35, 36, 71

T

Teacher Directors, 7
techniques, xiv, 3, 13, 19, 31, 34,
    43, 44, 48, 49, 56, 58, 69, 70, 71,
    72, 73, 83, 98, 119, 127
Tekena Mark, xiii, 20, 21, 23
tempo, 16, 29, 71
The Restoration Stage, 77
The System, xiv, 33, 37
Theatre, v, xiii, xiv, xv, 1, 2, 4, 8, 9,
    20, 21, 33, 37, 38, 43, 45, 51, 52,
    53, 54, 56, 58, 60, 63, 65, 67, 68,
    69, 70, 73, 74, 75, 76, 78, 79, 80,

85, 106, 115, 116, 120, 129, 130, 132, 133, 134, 135
theatre-in-the-round, 81, 98, 99, 104
Theatrical truth, 35
Theory, 5, 54
Thrust Stage, 93, 94, 95
Time, 28, 29
Traverse Stage, 97, 98
Trumbull, 14, 15, 16, 134
Tyrone Guthrie, 93

U

Uwatt, 4, 43, 44, 134

V

Vaux, 15, 134

verisimilitude, 9
Vertesi, 97, 98, 99, 134
Via Media theory, 53
Visual, 19
visual aesthetics, 19
Vsevolod Meyerhold, 9, 135

W

Wainstein, 83, 88, 89, 96, 134
Weight, 28, 29
workshopping method, 64
Worshipful approach, 14

Y

Yemi Ogunbiyi, 41

www.ingramcontent.com/pod-product-compliance
Lightning Source LLC
Chambersburg PA
CBHW050529270326
41926CB00015B/3131